Claim Your Surprise Gift

Thank you for purchasing my book. To show my appreciation, I've prepared a special gift for you that will help you sell more books. Access it by visiting:

www.albertgriesmayr.com/thank-you

★ Contents ★

★ NOTE FROM THE AUTHOR ★

"Marketing books successfully is hard. It takes knowledge and skills. Everyone who tells you differently has either been lucky, is unaware of the space, or isn't telling the truth."
Albert Griesmayr, 2020

My name is Albert Griesmayr, founder of the book publishing start-up Scribando | Novelify, which has helped thousands of writers sell more books over the last 10 years.

My passion is helping authors and publishers create phenomenal book projects based on solid setups and turbo-charged with amazing book marketing strategies. Over the last decade, I've personally worked with authors and publishers from more than 15 different countries, with book sales totalling more than 2 million copies worldwide. What I've learned is that creating successful book projects typically demands two things: (1) a solid, basic understanding of the drivers behind book marketing and (2) an awareness of the latest strategies and tactics.

My previous book, *Book Marketing Secrets*, is full of timeless insights that help create phenomenal book projects from the ground up.

The book you're currently reading is all about knowing and applying the latest ways to market your book. It contains my powerful and proven top 32 marketing tactics, which I use daily to help authors and publishers around the globe succeed.

I'm confident that each of the 32 tactics below has the power to double your book sales, regardless of whether you've been selling 5 copies a month or 500.

It seems like doubling or tripling your book sales would become harder when you're already in the high sales numbers, but I've often observed a surprising principle: the more successful a book already is, the more it actually benefits from applying premium tactics and strategies.

One reason for this is because successful books have already achieved a high level of good basic setup. These books are strong to begin with—they've been well thought out and well written, and they get good reviews and recommendations—so they benefit the most from advanced marketing tactics.

As I've mentioned, this book isn't about mastering the core setup. It's about spicing it up, adding those little secret ingredients to the marketing mix that make the difference between a good dish and a great one.

I hope you'll get as much value from the strategies and tactics in this book as I have from using them in my role as a consultant. Not only do I know every single tactic by heart, but I apply them all constantly when working with authors and publishers.

I wish you all the best in your career—and make sure to take a look at scribando.com and albertgriesmayr.com, where I share the latest insights on how to succeed in the fast-changing book publishing landscape as well.

Happy marketing. And never forget that marketing books successfully requires knowledge—knowledge you're holding in your hands right now.

Albert Griesmayr
Founder & CEO of Scribando | Novelify
January 1, 2021, Vienna, Austria

1 — INTRODUCTION
BOOK SALES EXPLOSION

A few weeks ago, I was chatting with the founder of one of Germany's fastest-growing Kindle book publishing businesses at the Frankfurt Book Fair. We were animatedly discussing the latest industry developments, such as audio-enabled conversations on Alexa and the impact AI will have on book writing. The conversation turned to the latest book marketing tactics on Amazon. Suddenly, we were exploring the seedy underworld of publishing.

This guy was giving me a deeper glimpse into the dark side of the industry, things I'd heard about but preferred not to contemplate: bots, advanced SEO, black-hat tactics, lawsuits, and much more. These things do not match the respectable, even glamorous, image of the publishing world, and I wish I were not aware of them—but sadly, they do exist.

Sitting at the Frankfurt Book Fair, surrounded by the most prestigious publishing houses and authors anywhere, it felt surreal to conjure up this dark world. But as we talked, it dawned on me that there's no escaping from this parallel world. It's part of the new reality. Welcome to digital book publishing!

Walking home that day, I reflected deeply on three questions:

1. Is my knowledge about book marketing tactics equally beneficial to all authors?

2. Is it okay to "help" authors or publishers with books when they're primarily looking to make a quick buck?

And lastly...

3. Where are we headed? Will there be a clash between traditional publishers and new players like Kindle or Audible, with their innovative and non-traditional methods?

Do not get the wrong idea. This book is essentially about helping you sell more books; it will not be a deep exploration of questions like these. But I am raising these issues because they have a direct bearing on what your book can achieve. The sections that follow introduce you to strategies that are guaranteed to benefit your book, whether it is something you have thrown your heart and soul into or a ghost written, profit-driven project meant to bring in cash.

So here is my take on the questions above:

1. Your book is the star. This is rule #1 of my Book Marketing Secrets. A good book can be a winner without good marketing, but a bad book cannot. Simple as that. But the flipside is that a bad book with good marketing can still get far. I have seen this numerous times in the market, not only in the digital world but also in the realm of print. Good marketing still moves products far and fast. Simply

enter a popular term—for example, "Keto Diet"—into your Amazon search bar, and you will find dozens of high-ranking books with the same basic content, the same look, and lots of reviews (many of them written, interestingly, in short timeframes). But many of those books do not add value. They were written by publishers more interested in keyword rankings than in creating a good read for their customers. And yes, it is all part of the game. But sooner or later, customers, as well as Amazon, will figure out which books deserve their attention and which ones do not. I am convinced that you can only "play the system" to a limited extent with a product that is not superior. And that is a good thing. Also, although there is still a long way to go and some people will always find ways to play the system, Amazon is becoming better and better at detecting and prioritizing truly valuable books.

That leads me to the second question:

2. As a book marketing consultant, I work with authors and publishers from around the world, and I do not always get to choose who I work with. I have often been confronted with books that lacked the quality I was hoping for. But over the years I have improved at sharing my honest perspective. Today, when an author or publisher hands me a book that does not provide additional value, I tell them so point-blank. Then I try to work with the client to improve the basics, primarily focusing on the book's quality. So, is it okay to help someone achieve best-selling status on Amazon when they might not deserve it? In general, yes—but first I always try to improve the book and help my clients develop and grow long-term in their craft. My approach

is the same in the book you are reading now. I cannot control how you will use the tips that follow, but I can control what I communicate and teach. So, let me be clear at the outset: success is ultimately about having a book you can be proud of, one that adds value to your target audience. This is what creates true satisfaction and makes every author happy at the end of the day. That sense of loving and taking pride in what you have created, in the impact you have achieved, is worth more than turning a quick buck anytime.

Regarding question number 3, I want to share my personal perspective with you. I have always felt more connected to the outliers in the publishing world than to traditional publishing houses. It all began when I launched my own start-up company, Scribando, around 10 years ago and reached out to traditional publishing houses to explain my concept. Quite honestly—and it happened more than once—some people made it clear they were not impressed.

You know that skeptical look, that feeling you sometimes get from an expert in your field, when you describe what you do? You can read it in their eyes: "You're not good enough. You're not part of the crowd." I still get this impression from time to time, even after having achieved some success and gained a little respect in the market.

Maybe I've been making the wrong connections, or maybe my impressions are off. In any case, I feel happier talking to outliers in the market, such as start-up founders, self-published authors, and service providers.

My sense is that there is still a substantial gap between these two groups that will not be easy to bridge in the near future. However, I hope that both communities will learn from each other—traditionalists from digital marketers about how to promote their books, and Kindle publishers from the traditional houses about how to create wonderful book projects.

* * *

To sum it all up, in my role as a book marketing consultant and CEO of the publishing start-up Scribando | Novelify, my main job is to help authors and publishing houses sell more books.

Achieving this goal requires not only a deep understanding of basic book marketing strategies but also an ability to stay on top of the latest insights and time-sensitive tactics in the market.

Staying current in both areas is difficult, even for people who do this full-time, because the market is extremely fast-paced—especially in digital book publishing.

One of the main reasons it is hard to keep up with the rate of change is that the digital world is not confined to specific sectors or industries. A change in the digital landscape has immediate effects on many industries, including traditionally slower-moving markets like the book industry. There is no escape from this trend. "Safe harbors" are increasingly rare in the book publishing business today.

Being able to succeed requires being alert and continuously up to date on the latest developments and strategies. With my start-up Scribando | Novelify, I focus on exactly that: keeping authors and publishers at the cutting edge of marketing.

As I mentioned earlier, my book *Book Marketing Secrets* offers timeless advice about how to sell more books. The one you are reading, however, includes the latest knowledge, the newest opportunities, and the most current and effective ways to market your book.

Here I share with you the 32 best book marketing tactics.

Most of these tactics are simple to understand, and if applied correctly, can have a huge impact on your book's performance. Do not try to add all the tactics to your marketing mix, though. Instead, focus on the ones that promise the best results for your specific setup and situation.

Based on my experience in digital book marketing, it is better to master 1–3 tactics and excel in your implementation than to apply 10 of the tactics poorly. In today's market, so many book marketers are screaming for attention that it is wiser not to scream louder but instead to scream differently, or to find alternative routes to reach your target audience.

* * *

My goal is for the tactics I share in this book to become as valuable to you as they have been to me and to hundreds of my clients around the world over the past several years. I am quite certain that each of the tactics in this book has the power to double your book sales, and that all of them combined have the power to triple them at the very least.

One way for me to measure the success of this book is if you get at least a 100% return on investment from purchasing it. In other words, if you spent $10 on it, I want you to make at least $20. Would you kindly send me an email or post a review letting me know if you hit that mark? I would love to hear about your experience of applying my tactics. Few things in life make me happier than seeing how my work helps authors and publishers and learning from their constructive feedback how to improve.

So, press forward—use the strategies in this book—and be a bold book marketer. Prove the effectiveness of these tactics in your own publishing journey.

Then my job with this book will have been a job well done.

★ 2 — TACTICS LIST OVERVIEW ★

Tactic	Summary	Hotness Factor
#1. Book Sales Funnel	Taking your visitors on a powerful marketing-oriented customer journey, from first contact to book purchase and potential upsells—quickly and effectively.	Fire!
#2. Look Inside / Reading Samples + Bonus Content	Including a visual in your book's first 10 pages that links to bonus content available on your webpage to get traffic.	Fire!
#3. The Truly Free Print Book	Offering a free print book and also covering shipping costs (targeted at limited editions & exclusive launches).	Super Hot
#4. Alexa Skills Book Promotion	Promoting books by creating related Alexa skills.	Super Hot
#5. Affiliate Marketing	Using Amazon and Audible affiliate programs (Audible Bounty & Amazon Affiliate) to increase book royalties.	Hot
#6. Translation & New Format Tactic	Increasing revenue and visibility by translating existing books and/or creating new formats.	Hot

Tactic	Summary	Hotness Factor
#7. Kickstarter Book Funding	Funding books on Kickstarter and applying pre-order strategies in general.	Super Hot
#8. Cialdinify Your Book	Spicing up your book marketing by applying Cialdini's principles from psychology to your approach.	Hot
#9. Permafree Ebook	Driving traffic to your author/ publisher webpage from a permafree ebook from online retailers.	Hot
#10. Cover/ Genre/Title Match Tactic	Matching book covers with the genre, title, and theme of books.	Hot
#11. Irresistible Bonus Offers	Spicing up the offer you make with your book by adding bonuses and creating irresistible packages and book offers.	Super Hot
#12. Pre-Order Tactic	Taking advantage of Amazon's expanded pre-order phase and BookBub's new release promo to give your book a powerful start.	Super Hot
#13. Amazon Bestseller Badge Tactic	Landing bestsellers on Amazon by focusing on short time spikes in non-competitive categories.	Hot
#14. Pinterest Traffic Generation	Getting traffic to your author webpage or Amazon sales page by leveraging Pinterest together with Tailwind Tribes.	Hot

Tactic	Summary	Hotness Factor
#15. Building an Author Platform with Email Marketing	Focusing on building a base of dedicated subscribers through email. (Get to 1,000!)	Hot
#16. Collaborative Book Promotion	Teaming up with other authors through legitimate review swapping, newsletter swapping, guest blogging, and Pinterest + Tailwind.	Hot
#17. Video Marketing on YouTube, Amazon & Beyond	Using video to tell your story to readers on YouTube, Amazon, Facebook, and other platforms.	Hot
#18. Amazon Select Price Promo + Discounted Book Service	Using discounted ebook alert services with a price promotion through Amazon KDP Select.	Hot
#19. Authority Book Publishing	Publishing a book with the primary goal of establishing authority and helping you reach higher-level business or career goals.	Hot
#20. Powerful Amazon SEO	Focusing on your top 1-3 keywords and rankings on Amazon and other major book retailers.	Hot
#21. Running Amazon Ads	Running ongoing Amazon Ads with a focus on book categories and/or keywords that you'll improve over time for maximum profitability.	Fire!

Tactic	Summary	Hotness Factor
#22. Audiobook Creation and Audiobook Giveaways	Releasing your book in an additional, fast-growing medium (audio) and supporting it with audiobook giveaways by using ACX, Findaway Voices, Audiobook Boom, and other services.	Super Hot
#23. Retargeting with Facebook Advertising + Messenger Marketing	Retargeting warm audiences to them engaged through Facebook ads and using Messenger marketing for viral campaigns or direct contact with fans.	Hot
#24. Kobo Publishing Tactic	Offering promotions through the smaller book retailer Kobo, where there's less competition and big sales opportunities.	Hot
#25. The Upsell Product Tactic (Infinite Selling Loops)	Getting profitable by always having another upsell product ready for your readers, like a companion course, personal coaching, or a book bundle/series.	Fire!
#26. Book Review Automation	Automating your book review process by offering a special bonus for feedback.	Super Hot
#27. Review Gathering with Pubby.co	Getting reviews with the help of Pubby.co	Fire!
#28. Using Librarybub	Reaching out to libraries with the help of Librarybub.	Hot
#29. Using Patreon	Patreon allows creators to build their userbases while getting paid at the same time	Hot

Tactic	Summary	Hotness Factor
#30. The Magic 100	Growing traffic and an influential network with The Magic 100	Fire!
#31. Running Cashback Campaigns	Running cashback campaigns in order to increase book rankings and to jumpstart sales algorithms.	Super Hot
#32. Google Play Promo Codes	Using promo code campaigns via Google Play.	Hot

Index Hotness Factor:

> Fire: 5x Potential

> Super Hot: 3x Potential

> Hot: 2x Potential

The Hotness Factor is primarily based on the potential return (80% relevance). The second factor it acknowledges is the cost of implementation in terms of time and money (20% relevance).

 # 3 — TACTIC DETAILS 

TACTIC 1

BOOK SALES FUNNEL

Description

A book sales funnel is a powerful marketing-oriented customer journey that quickly and effectively takes your visitors from first contact to book purchase and potential upsells.

Book sales funnels can range from simple to complicated. To create the simplest type of funnel, you must have the right mindset about what a funnel is, why it is beneficial, and how to design it effectively. A complicated funnel requires a comprehensive business visualisation with a clear understanding of the channels that bring traffic, the points of sale that convert traffic into paying customers, and systems of customer retention and activation.

Online sales funnels are especially important for selling books, since books are extremely competitive and do not have high profit margins. That is why it is critical to be able to convert traffic at healthy and profitable rates if you want your book business to work.

Examples of Success

Look at the following three main types of book funnels showcasing economically profitable book funnels. Consider how you could apply a book funnel to your own book business.

1) Free Print Book Funnels

Free print book funnels offer a free print copy; readers only pay for shipping.

Example: Russell Brunson—DotComSecrets

Russell Brunson (Founder of Clickfunnels) has reported multiple times that his book funnels were profitable, as he was able to pay for traffic with book sales at break-even, while being able to make profits from upsell products.

Thumbnail (January 31, 2019): https://dotcomsecrets.com

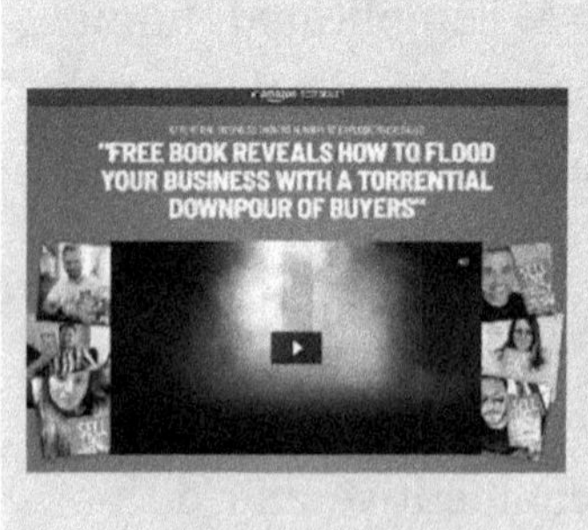

Example: Sabri Suby— Sell Like Crazy

Although we do not have reports directly from Sabri Suby about the profitability of his funnel, I suspect it works well based on the number of Amazon reviews and the ads running to the funnel for many months already.

Thumbnail (January 31, 2019): https://selllikecrazybook.com/

Example: Rob Kosberg— Publish, Promote, Profit

Rob Kosberg shares interesting insights on the performance of his funnel here: http://bestsellerpublishing.org/the-ins-outs-of-a-book-funnel/

Thumbnail (January 31, 2019): https://www.publishpromoteprofit.com/freebook

2) Paid eBook Funnels

Paid ebook funnels charge for an eBook directly at the point of sale and normally include upsells as well.

Example: Robert Neckelius—2 Hour Agency

Robert Neckelius sold an ebook for $4.95 upfront and had high-ticket coaching later. He was able to make the funnel profitable and cover most of his advertising costs with the book.

Thumbnail (January 31, 2019): https://2houragency.com/book/ +Insights: https://www.facebook.com/rneckelius/videos/721728171664333/

Example: Sean Vossler—7 Figure Marketing Copy

Sean Vossler successfully sold a package including an ebook for $37 total, as this campaign was running for a long time.

Thumbnail (January 31, 2019): https://app.increase.academy/most-important-skill-guide

3) Traffic-Oriented Book Funnels

Traffic-oriented book funnels have the primary target of driving traffic from online retailers, social media, or websites to other paid products, such as further books, digital courses, or affiliate products.

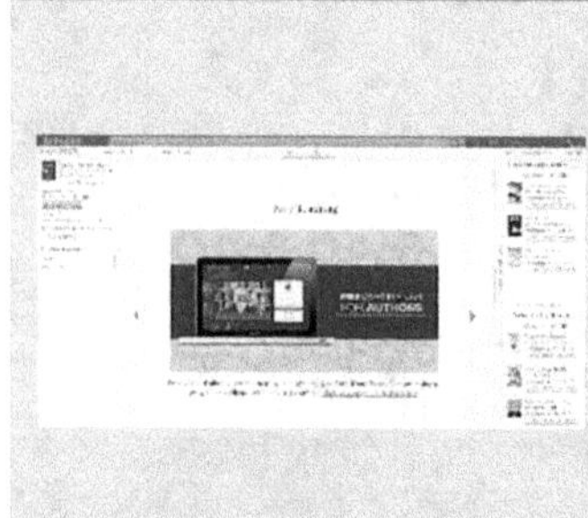

Example: Nick Stephenson—Reader Magnets

Nick Stephenson used a permafree book on Amazon to drive traffic to his webpage.

Thumbnail (January 31, 2019): https://amzn.to/2MBKZU3

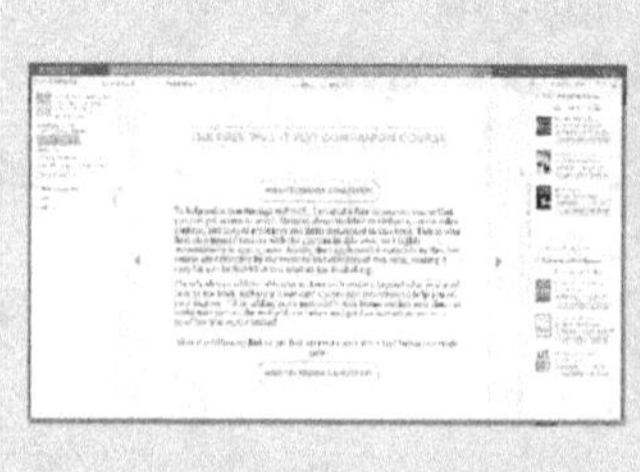

Example: Pat Flynn—Will It Fly?

Pat Flynn also used a permafree book on Amazon to drive traffic to his own products. According to Dave Chesson of Kindlepreneur, 30% of Pat's book buyers go on to access his Smart Passive Income course.

Thumbnail (January 31, 2019): https://amzn.to/3692D9I

Application

The first step in applying the funnel tactic is to keep the concept of a "funnel" itself at the front of your mind. It will change your mindset and enable you to make the right decisions. The easiest application is to add links from your book description or author bio to your webpage and to start thinking about upsells for your book.

The funnel strategy kicks in by creating a powerful, marketing-oriented book sales mechanism that quickly and effectively brings your visitors from first contact to book purchase and potential upsells. Equally important as the definition of the funnel steps and the funnel design (lead magnet, sign up, sale 1, sale 2, retention, etc.) is the choice of appropriate software.

Choosing the right software for your funnel is vitally important. You can design an incredible funnel on paper, but when it comes to execution, you will be largely dependent on your software capabilities and how quickly and effectively you can execute.

I recommend exploring Clickfunnels and Thrive Themes (the latter especially if you are using Wordpress), as well as Thrivecart, if you're primarily looking to integrate a powerful checkout process. When it comes to book fulfilment, and shipping free print books, look at Ship Your Books (shipyourbooks.com), Woocommerce (woocommerce.com), Amazon FBA, or local fulfilment providers.

Resources

> The Book Funnel: How to Go From Zero Audience to 6-Figure Business in One Book: https://fizzle.co/sparkline/book-funnel-zero-audience-to-6-figure-business

> Sales Funnel Strategy - 7 Simple Hacks To Get Your Sales Funnel To Convert: https://www.youtube.com/watch?v=Ip59Qbv6J_w

> Should I sell my book on Amazon or in a sales funnel? https://marketingsecrets.com/sell-book-amazon-sales-funnel/

> The Coaching/Consulting Book Sales Funnel: https://www.crazyeyemarketing.com/blog/the-coaching-consulting-book-sales-funnel-clickfunnels/

> The Ins and Outs of a Book Funnel: http://bestsellerpublishing.org/the-ins-outs-of-a-book-funnel/

> Mechanics behind free plus shipping funnels: https://www.clickfunnels.com/blog/mechanics-behind-free-plus-shipping-funnel/

TACTIC 2

USING AMAZON'S "LOOK INSIDE" AND READING SAMPLES TO COMMUNICATE BONUS CONTENT

Description

This tactic is all about creating enticing book intros and offers that can be included in a book's first couple of pages. Not only do these present the book favorably, but they also drive traffic by linking to bonus content available on external webpages.

Features like "look inside," "peek inside," or "reading samples" for download are a staple of most major online book retailers, often available for both ebooks and print books. In fact, it is a feature that readers have come to expect, and they use it frequently. It is natural for people to want to preview the content they're thinking of purchasing.

Optimizing and improving this content is a great tactic, and it can often be done easily by just working on a couple of pages and uploading a new version.

Examples of Success

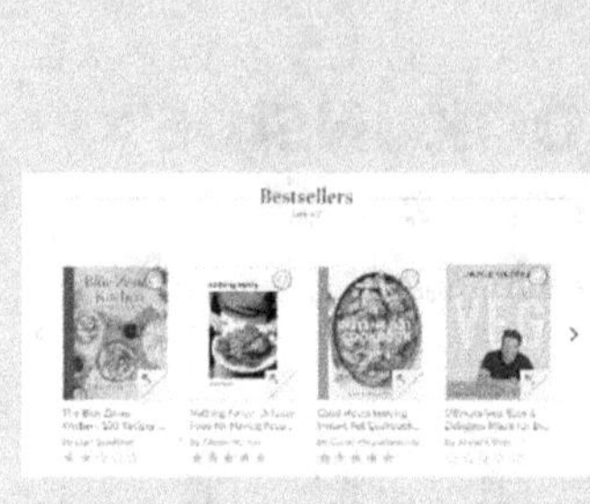

Example: Barnes & Noble—Look Inside / Reading Sample Feature

Look at Barnes & Noble's reading sample feature. It's highly used, so make sure your first 10 pages are enticing and, ideally, communicate value.

Thumbnail (January 8, 2020): https://bit.ly/2Frpt0y

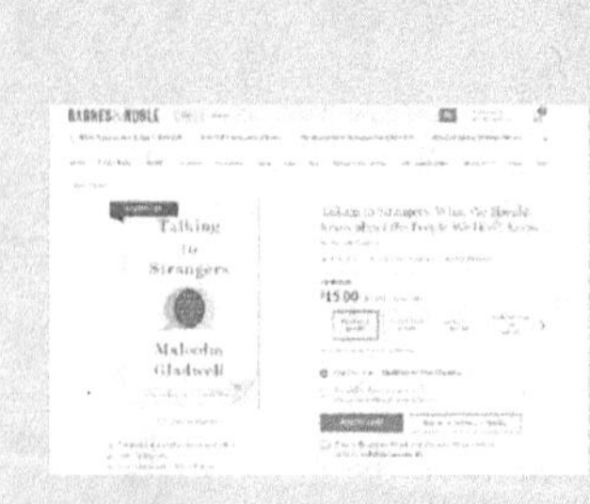

Example: Malcolm Gladwell—Talking to Strangers

Open the reading sample to see how the publisher is using the preview to advertise his book giveaways, sneak peeks, and other benefits by visiting his website.

Thumbnail (January 8, 2020): https://bit.ly/39OvGl8

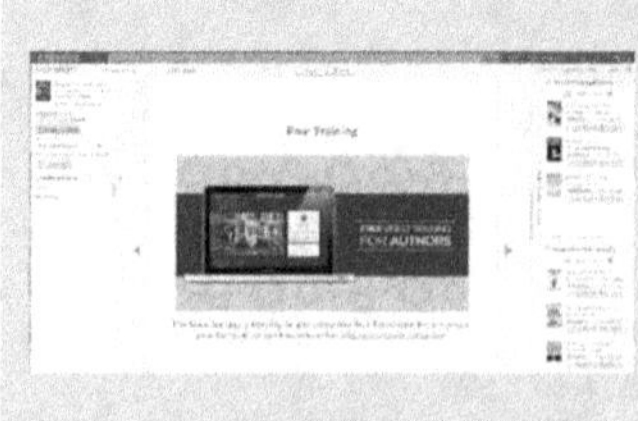

Example: Nick Stephenson—Reader Magnets

Nick Stephenson's Reader Magnets is another good example of using Amazon's "Look Inside" feature to show readers bonus content and drive traffic to a webpage.

Thumbnail (January 31, 2019): https://amzn.to/2MBKZU3

Application

Below you will find some low-hanging fruit, easy ways to work on your first couple of pages and your reading samples in order to optimize them (for higher conversion rates with book buyers) and drive traffic to your websites (for building email lists, selling further book titles and companion books, or presenting upsells).

Here are simple tips for optimizing:

> Copyright information and disclaimers: Reduce and/or move to the end of the book.

> Table of Contents: Design it neatly and attractively.

> Bonus content feature: Add a visual that catches the reader's attention, and include a big-font link to your webpage.

> Foreword / Note from the Author: Make it stand out. This section should still be promoting your book by listing benefits, or if it is a fiction book, by drawing readers into your story.

> Testimonials: Add them at the beginning to increase credibility.

If you're driving traffic to your webpage, you'll need to have enticing bonus content. Regardless of your specific niche, that content should add value. It could be a worksheet that complements the book, a market-specific report or analysis, a training video, or a free booklet or audiobook. Many authors also give away free ebooks of previous or upcoming releases.

Resources

> How to build an email list through Amazon:
> https://www.crazyegg.com/blog/build-list-through-amazon/

> Proven traffic strategies (Including getting traffic through Amazon):
> https://neilpatel.com/blog/7-proven-strategies-to-increase-your-blogs-traffic-by-206/#trafficstrategy1

TACTIC 3

THE TOTALLY FREE PRINT BOOK FUNNEL

Description

We have already discussed book funnels in Tactic #1. By now you are familiar with free print book funnels, which offer a print book for free, apart from shipping costs. This is a great tactic; not only are print books perceived as more valuable than ebooks because they are a physical item, but there are still loads of readers who prefer holding a good old-fashioned book in their hands and turning its pages. However, Tactic #3 goes one step further by offering a totally free print book that covers shipping as well.

How is this possible? How can you make it work financially?

This tactic relies on two ideas. First, you need to see the totally free print book as a marketing tactic aimed at generating buzz by making an exclusive offer to key target groups, such as influencers, journalists, or important beta readers. The goal is not to get a profit from the funnel itself, but to offer a limited number of copies for free (e.g., between 50 and 1,000) in exchange for something more valuable down the road—media attention, social media mentions, or a strong launch team built from enthusiastic readers.

Second, think of the funnel step as a way of bringing in leads who will purchase upsell products later, which will make the funnel profitable in the long run. This tactic is rarely used today, but it can be highly effective.

If you can master these two concepts and keep in mind the long-term benefits of offering a totally free print book, you'll have a very high chance of success.

Examples of Success

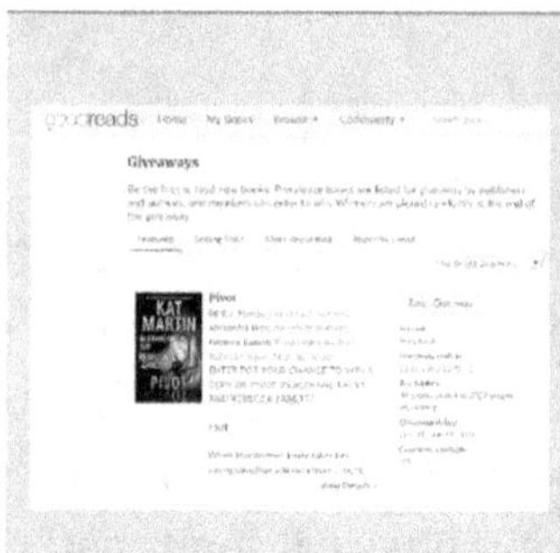

Example: Goodreads Giveaways

(Core idea: Giving away a limited number of free ARCs to create buzz and to secure feedback and reviews)

Thumbnail (January 10, 2020): https://www.goodreads.com/giveaway

Example: Cynthia L. Copeland—Win a copy of CUB

(Core idea: Giving away a limited number of free ARCs to create buzz and to secure feedback and reviews)

Thumbnail (January 10, 2020): https://bit.ly/2tInz8V

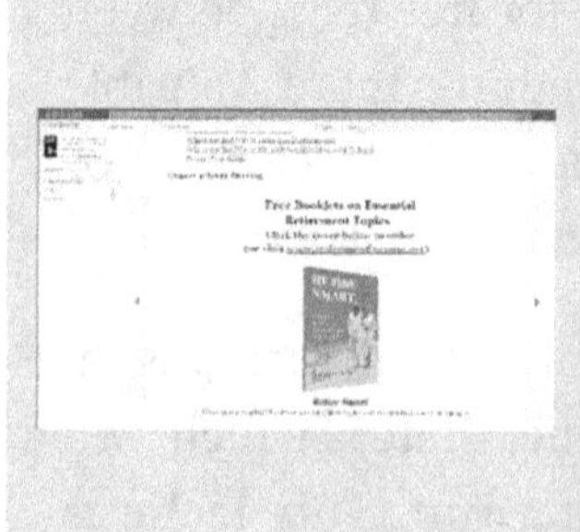

Example: Retirement Investing

(Core idea: Driving traffic from Amazon to landing pages, where you will offer a truly free print book, since lifetime value of customers is higher than print book + shipping costs)

Thumbnail (January 10, 2020): https://amzn.to/2Qzxxm5

Application

You can apply the "totally free print book" tactic either by limiting the offer in some way (normally by time, by number of copies, or to an exclusive audience) or by creating a totally free print book funnel with upsells. Find the most common applications below:

1) Pre-Launch/Pre-Order Package: The main goal is to generate interest among a target audience early. This could be achieved by creating a "secret landing page" that you only show to beta-readers, journalists, and influencers, where they can get a free copy shipped to them in exchange for signing up by email and joining a launch team.

2) Exclusive Audience Offer: Companies and authors in the industry with high-ticket clients apply this tactic to gain targeted readers, strengthen loyalty with existing customers, and build audiences. The free print book serves as a lead magnet, making it a profitable marketing tactic, since income from upsell products exceeds what you will spend on giving away the books for free.

3) Book Launch & Readings: Book launches, book giveaways, and readings are also a good practical application, provided there are upsell products available to compensate for the upfront expense.

Resources

> How to Maximize Goodreads Giveaways for Better Engagement:
> https://www.amarketingexpert.com/maximize-goodreads-giveaways/

> How to Use Boost Book Sales With Advanced Reader Copies (ARCs):
> https://www.authormedia.com/155/

> How to Get Books Before They're Published:
> https://bookriot.com/2018/08/17/how-to-get-books-before-theyre-published/

TACTIC 4

ALEXA SKILLS BOOK PROMOTION

Description

The main idea behind Tactic #4 is to use Amazon Alexa-enabled devices as a channel for promoting books and related services. Amazon Alexa is a colossal investment by the company. By November 2018, Amazon had more than 10,000 employees working on Alexa and related products. As of January 2019, Amazon's devices team announced that they had sold over 100 million Alexa-enabled devices. It's one of the fastest-growing market phenomena, closely related to audiobooks because of its voice technology and to the purchase of other products on Amazon, such as books, due to its integration with the company's ecommerce business.

The Alexa Skill Book Promotion Tactic certainly launches you into a fresh field, but one that offers high rewards for publishers with existing audiences to tap—especially if you are willing to put a little energy into creating an amazing Alexa skill and marketing it effectively.

Examples of Success

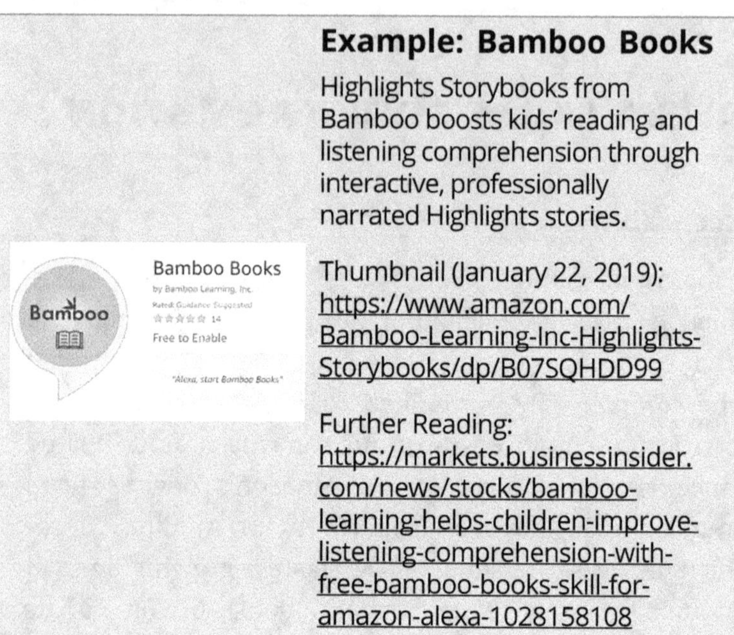

Example: Bamboo Books

Highlights Storybooks from Bamboo boosts kids' reading and listening comprehension through interactive, professionally narrated Highlights stories.

Thumbnail (January 22, 2019): https://www.amazon.com/Bamboo-Learning-Inc-Highlights-Storybooks/dp/B07SQHDD99

Further Reading: https://markets.businessinsider.com/news/stocks/bamboo-learning-helps-children-improve-listening-comprehension-with-free-bamboo-books-skill-for-amazon-alexa-1028158108

Example: The Magic Door

This story-based game, driven by Alexa, lets readers shape the plot by making choices.

Thumbnail (January 22, 2019): https://www.amazon.com/The-Magic-Door-LLC/dp/B01BMUU6JQ/

https://www.themagicdoor.org/stories/

Alexa Skills are not limited to particular books. The examples above are just a glimpse of what is possible in fiction by bringing stories to Alexa in an engaging, interactive way.

Application

There are numerous practical applications when it comes to promoting your book on Alexa. Amazon Alexa makes it easy to create a skill for non-developers as well, by using Alexa Skill Blueprints (https://blueprints.amazon.com/). You can create quizzes, games, stories, and much more. Developers can even work with in-app purchases that allow customers to buy your ebook on Amazon Kindle through Alexa.

Another very promising, largely untapped field is the re-use of existing audiobooks (and podcasts) on Alexa. Opportunities are rapidly expanding! To get started, I suggest visiting Alexa Skill Blueprints and exploring the options. Make sure you also read up on the latest developments and best practices. One example of low-hanging fruit is to simply take advantage of what Alexa can already do with Kindle books: read your book aloud.

Thumbnail (January, 10, 2020): Amazon Alexa Skills Blueprints, https://blueprints.amazon.com

The most critical step in using Alexa Skills is being proactive about promotion. Unfortunately, if you publish a skill today without any marketing, the chances of someone finding it are slim. Like any other product on the internet, it needs to be promoted. If you are going to publish an Alexa skill to promote your book, make sure you already have an audience or marketing steps in place. If your skill becomes popular, the rewards can be high.

Resources

> How to market Alexa Skills:
https://blog.hubspot.com/marketing/alexa-skills-marketing

> Ways to increase your Amazon Alexa audience:
https://medium.com/effct-voice/7-awesome-ways-to-increase-your-amazon-alexa-audience-right-now-fb22040ba20d

> How to promote your Alexa skill:
https://onlim.com/en/how-to-promote-your-amazon-alexa-skill/

> The 60 most useful Alexa skills of 2020:
https://www.lifewire.com/alexa-skills-4126799

> Publisher Capstone to bring children's book bundles to Alexa subscribers:
https://www.publishersweekly.com/pw/by-topic/childrens/childrens-industry-news/article/79505-capstone-brings-children-s-book-bundles-to-alexa-subscribers.html

TACTIC 5

AFFILIATE MARKETING

Description

Affiliate Marketing starts with a mindset—a mindset of looking further than your own nose (and your products) and imagining things from the client's perspective. How can your clients get the best possible value?

This mindset changes your whole approach. You automatically start noticing the best products of other marketers and thinking about how to incorporate them when offering your own products, giving advice, or interacting with other people.

Luckily, the internet has made it relatively easy to get little financial rewards for recommending others' products and making referrals. That is what affiliate marketing is all about.

For authors and publishers, affiliate marketing starts with Amazon. When you become an Amazon affiliate, you add links on your personal website that will lead your audience to useful products on Amazon. You can, of course, promote others' products, but you can also link to your own books! When someone follows a link and makes a purchase, you make money.

But if you are a business-minded author, affiliate marketing does not need to stop with Amazon. Audible also has a fantastic affiliate program and skilled marketers.

One caveat: This tactic works best for authors and publishers with an established audience since affiliate marketing requires substantial site traffic to really become profitable. So, make sure you have already built an audience before investing too much time in an affiliate marketing strategy.

Examples of Success

Example: A. D. Starrling

Author A. D. Starrling uses Amazon affiliate links to send readers from her webpage to her books. The string of text at the end of the URL (right image, highlighted for illustration) shows that an affiliate tag has been placed.

See affiliate links to her popular book series: https://www.adstarrling.com/division-eight/

Thumbnail (February 20, 2020): https://www.adstarrling.com/division-eight/

Example: Debbie Drum

Debbie Drum, the face behind the popular review software Book Review Targeter and bestselling author of Read Better, Faster, is also a power affiliate marketer. She regularly shares others' products in her newsletter. Sometimes a single newsletter brings her thousands of dollars in affiliate commissions.

Thumbnail (January 21, 2020): https://publisherrocket.com/affiliate-program/

Application

> There is a simple first step if you currently do not have much traffic: sign up for Amazon Affiliates and use the affiliate link to send readers to your own book. You will begin earning a little commission.

> Next, use the Amazon affiliate link whenever you are promoting others' products on your website. Visit https://affiliate-program.amazon.com/ to get started.

> If you have an audiobook on Audible published through ACX, make sure you look at their Bounty Referral Program. You can make as much as $75 every time someone gets an Audible membership because they bought your audiobook through your referral link.

> Tips for pro marketers:

> Check out popular affiliate networks like Clickbank, which enable you to do even more.

> Reach out to related businesses and strike a deal—see if they are willing to collaborate through newsletter swapping, social media mentions, or direct promotion of your books and products.

Resources

> How To Guide: Affiliate Marketing:
> https://www.youtube.com/watch?v=eJkqtLPymQs

> Amazon Affiliate Marketing for Beginners:
> https://www.youtube.com/watch?v=kMZ92_jzhOo

> Why You Should Be an Amazon Affiliate If You Are
> an Author:
> https://justpublishingadvice.com/why-you-need-to-be-
> an-amazon-affiliate-if-you-are-an-author/

TACTIC 6

TRANSLATIONS AND NEW FORMATS

Description

So, you have published a book that sells. Congratulations! Now what is your next target?

Selling it as often as possible, no doubt. You want to double down on sales and get an edge in the market. But what is the best strategy?

Oftentimes it is creating new formats and translations. Compared to the labor involved in creating totally new books and products, it is easy to make a new iteration of something you have already had success with. Some examples would be turning a paperback book into an ebook, a print book into an audiobook, or an English bestseller into Spanish, German, or French. These are low-hanging fruit.

Moreover, if you use a freelancer platform like Upwork or Fiverr, you can keep your costs down by working with freelancers or agencies that offer more competitive pricing. Some will create translations or new formats of your book for only a few hundred dollars.

Examples of Success

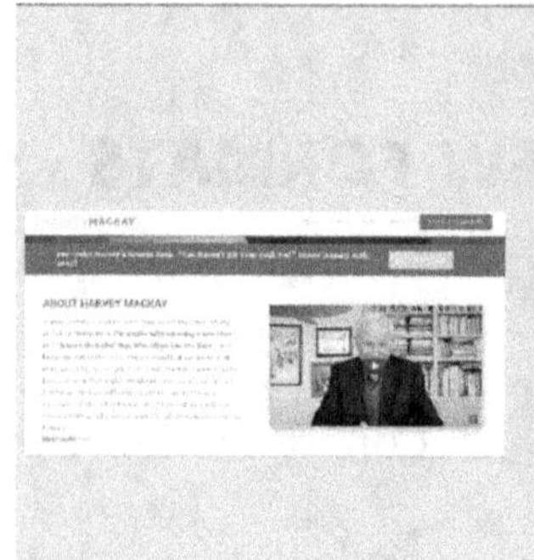

Example: Harvey Mackay

Bestselling authors like Harvey Mackay have made huge profits from translations. According to Mackay's website, "Harvey's books have sold 10 million copies worldwide, been translated into 46 languages and have sold in 80 countries."

Thumbnail (January 21, 2020): https://harveymackay.com/

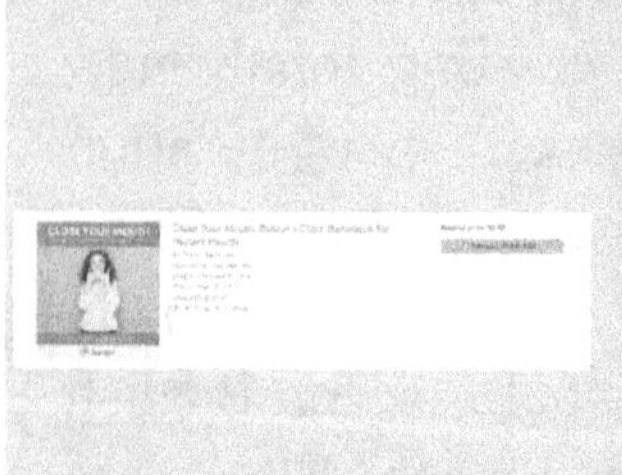

Example: Patrick McKeown

Successful Irish writer and medical practitioner Patrick McKeown turned his bestseller Close Your Mouth into an audiobook. The new version immediately opened a powerful income stream, attracting customers who preferred an audio format to reading.

Thumbnail (January 21, 2020): Audible https://www.audible.com/author/Patrick-McKeown/B006X1OD3U

Application

Creating a new format for your book—e.g., audiobook, hardcover, paperback, or ebook—is remarkably easy through Amazon's self-publishing services. Translating your book into another popular language can also tap into an untapped audience, bringing in new profits (see below for resources on translation).

Resources

> How to Get Your Book Translated:
> https://kindlepreneur.com/book-translation/

> How to Make an Audiobook Step-by-Step:
> https://self-publishingschool.com/creating-audiobook-
> every-author-know/

TACTIC 7

KICKSTARTER BOOK FUNDING

Description

Kickstarter is a crowdfunding platform with enormous potential for authors and publishers—but it is often overlooked. Use Kickstarter's publishing section to create amazing projects, pre-fund your book, and implement a smart pre-order strategy.

Kickstarter provides a great model of "lean publishing," or publishing that does not require huge capital or a lengthy, complicated process to get your book into the hands of readers. It also offers significant advantages over the traditional publishing model. For example, you can share your ideas with followers, build a fanbase early, plan a promotional campaign, and get feedback on the development of your book before you even write a single chapter. The examples in the section below became publishing sensations on Kickstarter, raising hundreds of thousands of dollars from tens of thousands of supporters.

Check out kickstarter.com and browse other book projects to see what is possible. The support you get while writing your masterpiece could be priceless.

Examples of Success

Example: Hello Ruby

Hello Ruby is a children's book that teaches the basics of programming in a fun and engaging way. As the screenshot above shows, author Linda Liukas raised far more than her stated funding goal from enthusiastic backers

Thumbnail (January 24, 2020): Linda Liukas, Hello Ruby, https://www.kickstarter.com/projects/lindaliukas/hello-ruby

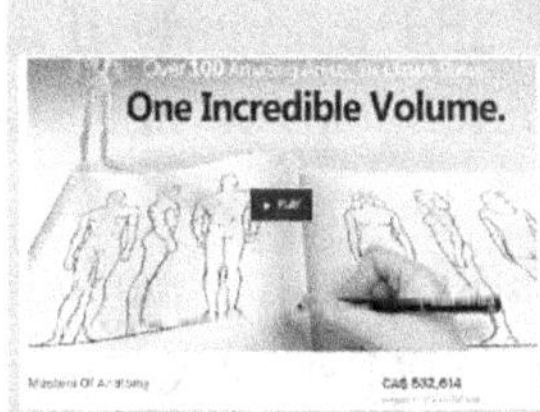

Example: Masters of Anatomy

Masters of Anatomy is a collaborative book by dozens of artists, designed to be a reference work for modern illustrators and comic book artists. As you can see from the funding bar (above), the Idea was wildly popular.

Thumbnail (January 24, 2020): Masters of Anatomy, Master of Anatomy: The Ideal Male and Female, https://www.kickstarter.com/projects/1302528630/masters-of-anatomy

Example: The Leader's Guide

Entrepreneur and author Eric Ries built on his successful "Lean Startup" principles to launch a book project on Kickstarter. The pitch was well received by thousands of business leaders who had benefited from Ries's ideas.

Thumbnail (January 24, 2020): Eric Ries, The Leader's Guide, https://www.kickstarter.com/projects/881308232/only-on-kickstarter-the-leaders-guide-by-eric-ries

Application

Publishing on Kickstarter can save you lots of time, money, and energy. Publish the lean way and find out early if your target audience is interested in your book (or not). They will let you know through their funding support. Similarly, use Kickstarter to test your marketing approach and identify what resonates with your prospective readers. Build an audience early so you can hit the ground running with your book release.

Resources

❯ 8 Lessons for Launching Your Book with Kickstarter: https://scribewriting.com/8-lessons-for-launching-your-book-with-a-kickstarter-and-raising-25000/

❯ Creator Handbook: https://www.kickstarter.com/help/handbook. How does my project become a Project We Love?: https://help.kickstarter.com/hc/en-us/articles/115005135214-How-does-my-project-become-a-Project-We-Love-

TACTIC 8

CIALDINIFY YOUR BOOK

Description

When it comes to attracting and converting potential readers, few things matter more than your book offers or book descriptions. They need to be awesome. Every word adds spice to the "dish," making the content appealing to prospective buyers.

I take my ingredients for spicing up offers and book descriptions from well-known psychologist Robert Cialdini. His classic book on persuasion and influence describes 6 principles: reciprocity, consistency, social proof, liking, authority, and scarcity. (A seventh principle, "unity," was added in 2016.) I personally use these principles like salt and pepper in my own marketing. Taken together, they are a powerful arsenal for any marketer.

Check out the examples of Cialdini principles in action below and read my tips for how you can season your own marketing with these powerful persuasion tactics.

Examples of Success

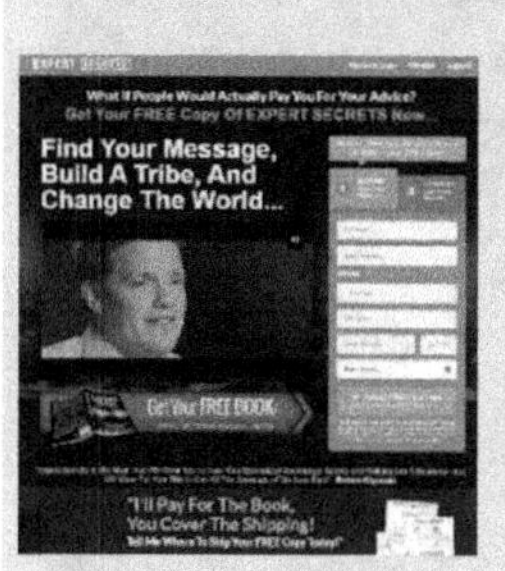

Example (plus a quick exercise):

The book sales page of Expert Secrets by Russell Brunson: How many of Cialdini's principles can you find?

Thumbnail (January 30, 2020): https://expertsecrets.com/freebook

Solution: If you look over the whole sales page, you'll see that Russell actually uses all of Cialdini's principles. In the screenshot above, he uses reciprocity (offering a free book), social proof (providing a testimonial), and authority and liking (with a video).

Example: Bad Blood: *Secrets and Lies in a Silicon Valley Startup* by John Carreyrou

This Amazon sales page uses credibility (listing awards) and authority ("prize-winning journalist") heavily to create a compelling book description and subsequent offer.

Thumbnail (January 30, 2020): Amazon, https://www.amazon.com/Bad-Blood-Secrets-Silicon-Startup-ebook/dp/B078VW3VM7

Application

Find my concrete applications for each Cialdini principle below.

Principle	Application
Reciprocity	❯ Give your readers something valuable (for free) first to trigger "reciprocity" in return (this can even be used in descriptions by sharing a valuable insight or quote early on in your book description or offer). ❯ Before making your offer, tell your readers what you've already done for them (this works well if you've already provided value, e.g., with the delivery of a lead magnet).
Consistency	❯ Get your readers to commit by signing up or reading part 1 of your series. ❯ Remind your readers of the specific goals your book can help them with ("You want to reach X, so read the book").
Social Proof	❯ Use testimonials and reviews to highlight what other readers liked about your book.
Liking	❯ Present yourself, as the author, in the best possible light. Use pictures/videos on Author Central where you're on a stage. Share audience numbers, like number of YouTube subscribers. Show reviews of your work by popular, respected figures.
Authority	❯ Make sure your offers, book descriptions, and author biography include details that establish your credentials, experience, and recognition. What makes you qualified to write this book?

Principle	Application
Scarcity	❯ Give your readers a sense of urgency and priority. Limit your offer in some way to incentivize engagement—for example, through an early-bird bonus for the first 100 readers.
Unity	❯ Connect with your readers on a deeper level by creating a shared identity around your book and subject—e.g., based on location, traits, personal interests, or challenges.

Resources

❯ Robert Cialdini. Influence: The Psychology of Persuasion (1984): https://www.amazon.com/Influence-Psychology-Persuasion-Robert-Cialdini/dp/006124189X

❯ Cialdini's 7th Persuasion Principle: Using Unity in Online Marketing: https://cxl.com/blog/cialdini-unity/

❯ How to Use Cialdini's 6 Principles of Persuasion to Boost Conversions: https://cxl.com/blog/cialdinis-principles-persuasion/

❯ Dr. Robert Cialdini: The Psychology Powering Influence and Persuasion [podcast]: https://guykawasaki.com/dr-robert-cialdini-the-godfather-of-influence/

TACTIC 9

PERMAFREE EBOOK

Description

Driving traffic from a book to a webpage is a potent way to grow your audience. Tactic #9 uses a related tool: offering a free ebook as a magnet for readers.

Free ebooks are not a new concept in and of themselves. But as with so many things, it is all about context. When you offer a free ebook on a platform where content is not usually free—e.g., through a book retailer like Amazon, or as an exclusive download on a file-sharing website— perceived value for readers increases. If you can lead them from an ebook to your webpage, you will boost site traffic and ultimately your sales.

The examples below show several ways you can leverage this tactic.

Examples of Success

The core idea in examples 1 and 2, below, is offering a free ebook / print book, or a "Look Inside" bonus (often an exclusive or limited time offer), in order to drive traffic to the author's website, combined with upsells in the back.

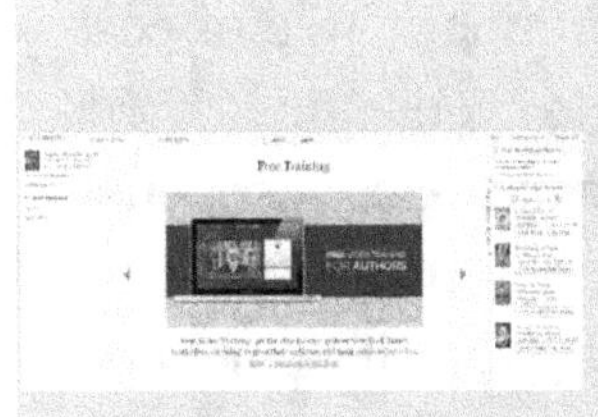

Example: Nick Stephenson, Reader Magnets

Drive traffic from a permafree ebook on Amazon to your website.

Thumbnail (February 20, 2020): https://www.amazon.com/Reader-Magnets-Platform-Marketing-Authors-ebook/dp/B00PCKIJ4C

Example: Tim Ferriss, "4-Hour Chef"

Use BitTorrent to generate interest in a special pre-release package.

Thumbnail (February 20, 2020): https://now.bt.co/bundles/651c-d5ae832b9607eb35b394708b-f8c5c5245f5a0573a64e93c4e-b87364eeeae

Example: Russell Brunson, The Marketing Secrets Blackbook

Brunson uses a free ebook to build authority and drive traffic to ClickFunnels, his software company and upsell service.

Thumbnail (February 20, 2020): https://marketingsecrets.com/blackbook

Application

> Offer readers a free ebook by distributing it free of cost to online book retailers. Stores like Apple and Kobo accept permafree ebooks. Although Amazon does not accept permafree ebooks at the moment, until recently it supported price matching, meaning that if your book is set to $0.00 on another major bookseller's website, Amazon will set its price to $0.00 to match.

> Alternatively, make Permafree ebooks a key part of your funnel strategy, to draw readers from the ebook to your personal webpage. Another way to do this is to bypass online book retailers. Instead, simply upload your ebook as a PDF to your webpage. Google search engines favor PDFs, and you might be surprised at how many hits your book gets through basic Google searches. Of course, it helps if you already have a core audience, and your book should have an SEO-smart title.

> If you create an exclusive limited time offer, prospective readers are even more likely to visit your webpage to take advantage of the free ebook.

> If you use the popular Kindle Direct Publishing (KDP) on Amazon, you can also enroll in KDP Select and run a "Free Book Promotion" for up to 5 days to make your book available to readers at no cost during that period.

Resources

> Get more insights from my presentation "Book Sales Funnels," available through the link below: https://docs.google.com/presentation/d/e/2PACX-1vTrL-nmehyAlIMK-w92wR-GHKDuzJQ272UJNAwtM Fqb6nAwWeohA24OmfgkuUoPoS3Afg-zoKGTSrGV/ pub?start=false&loop=false&delayms=3000

> Making my Book Free on Amazon and Other Book Stores: https://loganbrookfield.com/2019/03/making-my-book-free-on-amazon-and-other-book-stores/

> How to Build Your Marketing List Through the Amazon Kindle Store: https://www.crazyegg.com/blog/build-list-through-amazon/

TACTIC 10

THE KILLER BOOK COVER TACTIC

Description

Even though we all know the old saying, we cannot help judging books by their covers. Typography, title, and design send a powerful message to our brain, quickly telling us whether a book is worth our time—or not. For us authors and publishers, it is crucial to design a cover that will make readers want to see what is inside and ultimately buy the book. Designing a good cover can be hard, but you can succeed by applying the "magic book cover formula" to create a killer book cover.

Magic Book Cover Formula:
Genre Match + Title/Visual Match + Benefits +
Unique Twists = Resulting Wow Effect

The four things you need to keep in mind are "genre matching," "title matching," "communicating benefits," and "uniqueness to stand out." I will explain each of these through examples below.

In the end, your cover should survive the test question, "Is my cover a killer book cover? Is my cover truly awesome?" If you can answer yes, you have done a great job.

Examples of Success

Example: Classic Business Book Designs (Cover/Genre Matching + Benefits)

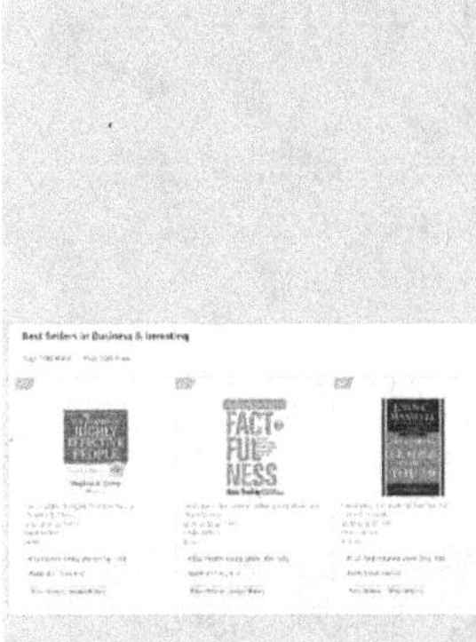

Note the large title fonts and the sparing use of background images in these business covers. There's also a heavy focus on communicating the benefits of the book, something that's super important for non-fiction books

Thumbnail (February 20, 2020): https://www.amazon.com/Best-Sellers-Kindle-Store-Business-Investing/zgbs/digital-text/154821011/ref=zg_bs_nav_kstore_2_154606011

Example: Classic Romance Book Designs (Cover/Genre/Title Matching)

These romance covers all use subtle, warm imagery. Glendy Vanderah's Where the Forest Meets the Stars, especially, shows brilliant title/cover matching. The cover stands out. It's unique.

Thumbnail (February 20, 2020): https://www.amazon.com/Best-Sellers-Kindle-Store-Romance/zgbs/digital-text/158566011/ref=zg_bs_nav_kstore_2_154606011

Example: Classic Mystery, Thriller & Suspense Book Designs (Cover/Genre Matching)

A pattern in the Mystery, Thriller & Suspense bestseller covers above is big-font author names and mysterious imagery. Dean Koontz's In the Heart of the Fire also shows magnificent title/cover matching—there's no mistaking what kind of book it is, and the cover itself isn't like to be confused with others. It has a unique twist.

Thumbnail (February 20, 2020): https://www.amazon.com/Best-Sellers-Kindle-Store-Mystery-Thriller-Suspense/zgbs/digital-text/157305011

Finally, see below two examples of covers with a unique twist.

Phil Knight's _Shoe Dog_ clearly stands out by using the iconic Nike sign on the cover.

Thumbnail (February 20, 2020): https://www.amazon.com/Shoe-Dog-Memoir-Creator-Nike-ebook/dp/B0176M1A44

Donna Tartt's _The Goldfinch_ jumps out by adding a 3-D element to the cover.

Thumbnail (February 20, 2020): https://www.amazon.com/Goldfinch-Donna-Tartt-ebook/dp/B00C74SHRK

Application

Apply the magic book cover formula to your book. Make sure it has the following four qualities:

1. Genre Match. First, a book's cover should clearly communicate the genre it belongs to. If you browse bestsellers in your genre, you'll notice consistent aesthetic trends. Your book should follow suit. By matching the main design elements of the genre—like trim size, fonts, and visuals—you not only accurately meet readers' expectations but also align with proven selling indicators for your type of book. Bestselling how-to books always look crisp, current, and straightforward. Bestselling romance novels always look dreamy, intimate, and inviting. If you want readers to open your book, it is wise to match the cover with the genre.

2. Visual/Title Match. You will want to carefully match your visuals with your title. Authors know that the title should reflect the book's contents, but equally important is to make sure the title and the cover design are in harmony. Take this book, for example: *Book Sales Explosion.* If I had used an image of something calm or peaceful, not something explosive, it would have miscommunicated the idea behind the title. That kind of mismatch can be jarring, ultimately turning away prospective readers. So, when you are designing your cover, consider whether your title and your visuals are really saying the same thing.

3. Communicating Benefits. Make sure your book communicates what is in it for readers. Title and subtitle matter the most in this, but the overall book design also plays an important role. Adding credibility to covers also conveys the benefits to readers. You can do this by adding powerful testimonials from established authors and professionals, and by displaying on the cover the awards and achievements your book can already claim.

4. Uniqueness. Outstanding covers have one element that makes them unique. Find the one element that will make your cover unique and add it. Often this one unique element has a profound impact on your book's performance.

A final tip is to check out the bestsellers in your genre on Amazon. Pay attention to trends in the covers, such as color scheme, fonts and font size, visuals, how the author's name appears, and the interplay between text and image. Now go back to your cover draft: how does it compare to the bestsellers? Consider the design elements as well as the title. Make sure everything matches!

In the end, you need to be able to look at your book cover and say it is awesome. It is a simple but effective test!

Resources

> The Impact a Book Cover Has on Sales:
> https://en.99designs.at/blog/tips/impact-book-cover-design-on-sales/

> How to Design a Book Cover Based on Its Genre:
> https://blog.flipsnack.com/how-to-design-a-book-cover-based-on-its-genre/

> The Complete Guide to Choosing Your Book Cover Font with Examples:
> https://blog.publishdrive.com/book-cover-font-guide/

TACTIC 11

IRRESISTIBLE BONUS OFFERS

Description

Every pro marketer knows that one of the best things you can do to sell your book is make an irresistible offer.

Ideally your book will already be irresistible—but competition is fierce. You might be up against dozens or even hundreds of books in your category, and it can be difficult to stand out and show the value your book offers.

That is where the irresistible bonus offer comes in, adding value to the book purchase for prospective buyers and giving you a competitive edge. Classic examples of irresistible bonus offers are companion courses, included memberships, and bonus ebooks.

It is important not only to have an irresistible bonus offer but also to feature this prominently in your first few pages and in your book descriptions at online retailers like Amazon.

Examples of Success

Example: Albert Griesmayr landing page

You can use a landing page to create an enticing offer. I did this by offering a free read of my books to the first 1,000 persons who joined my book launch team.

Thumbnail (February 10, 2020): https://www.albertgriesmayr. com/launch-team

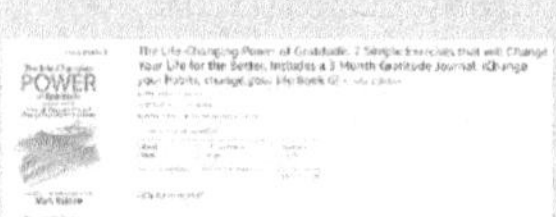

Example: Amazon sales page for The Life-Changing Power of Gratitude

Notice how the line "Includes a 3 Month Gratitude Journal" appears in the subtitle on the sales page, instantly attracting prospective buyers.

Thumbnail (February 10, 2020): https://www.amazon.com/ Life-Changing-Power-Gratitude- Exercises-Journal-ebook/dp/ B07KW132ZL

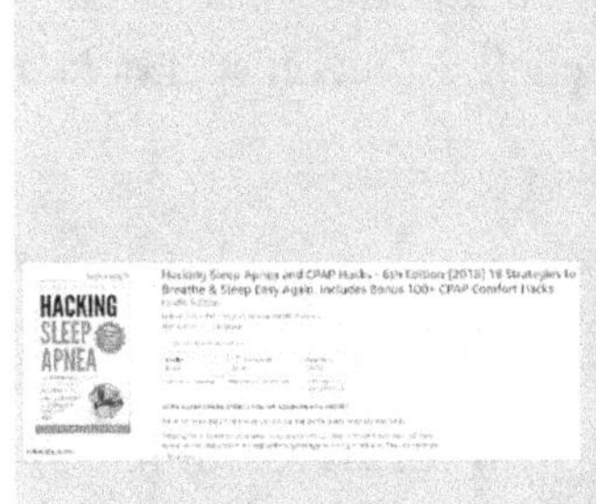

Example: Amazon sales page for Hacking Sleep Apnea

Again, this sales page shrewdly advertises the bonus in the subtitle: "Includes Bonus 100+ CPAP Comfort Hacks."

Thumbnail (February 10, 2020): https://www.amazon.com/Hacking-Sleep-Apnea-CPAP-Hacks-ebook/dp/B01BU9U6OE

Application

> Brainstorm ways to create an irresistible bonus offer with your book. Also, consider whether it will be sustainable and scalable—for example, you would not be able to offer free coaching calls for every reader, as this would quickly become too time-consuming and quite unprofitable.

> Some commonly used bonus offers you can use are companion courses, additional ebooks, website memberships, and adding purchasers to an exclusive email list.

> The perceived value of your bonus offer also matters. I recommend creating a bonus worth at least twice the price of the book. Companion courses become highly attractive for readers when you can offer content with a theoretical value of $37 or more.

> Finally, make sure your readers pay attention to your bonus offer. The best way to do this is to include it in your book description. Another good place to add

it is in the first few pages of the book, since potential buyers will see this when they click Amazon's "Look Inside" preview.

Resources

> How to Sell Anything to Anyone with an Irresistible Offer:
> https://www.youtube.com/watch?v=AbDMNSfOY6c

> How to Craft an Irresistible Offer:
> https://www.digitalmarketer.com/blog/how-to-craft-an-irresistible-offer/

> How to Sell A Product — Sell Anything to Anyone with The 4 S's Method:
> https://www.youtube.com/watch?v=jsPYqsnJgf4

TACTIC 12

PRE-ORDER TACTIC

Description

If you want your book to hit the ground running, you should make the most of the pre-launch phase. This is the time to generate buzz, get feedback, recruit beta readers, and secure potential reviews. You can even monetize the process by getting pre-orders through online retailers like Barnes & Noble or Amazon.

This tactic has proven increasingly effective over the last few years, and with new developments at the start of 2020, it is going to become even more valuable. The two big trends are (1) Amazon extending its pre-order phase up to one year and (2) BookBub offering submissions for featured new release promotion (which have less competition than the featured discounted book deals).

Amazon's new allowance means that you can not only "claim" a future release one year in advance but also rack up pre-orders far ahead of the launch. If used correctly, it can also act as pre-funding. A good approach is to offer special pre-order packages exclusively for readers who pre-order the book.

Examples of Success

Example: Why Not Me?

Mindy Kaling's second book, Why Not Me?, was launched at #1 on the New York Times bestseller list. The pre-publication phase included a gift-with-pre-order promotion consisting of her favorite licorice and a Why Not Me? pin to readers who pre-ordered the book.

Thumbnail (February 10, 2020): Emerald City Glow, http://www.emeraldcityglow.com/2015/08/19/hump-day-happiness-preorder-gift-from-mindy-kaling/

Example: Julia Ember giveaway

Julia Ember invited readers to forward pre-order receipts by email in exchange for a simple pre-order giveaway.

Thumbnail (February 10, 2020): A Marketing Expert, https://www.amarketingexpert.com/the-13-pre-order-strategies-that-increase-book-sales/

Example: BookBub pre-order alert and campaign by author Kathryn Le Veque

Kathryn Le Veque used BookBub to get publicity and pre-orders for the first book in her popular Warwolfe series.

Thumbnail (February 10, 2020): BookBub, https://insights.bookbub.com/promoted-preorder-launch-bestselling-book/

Application

❯ Make your book available for pre-order on your own sales page or through online retailers (like Amazon and Barnes & Noble) long before the release date.

❯ Create an enticing pre-order package that will clearly reward readers who pre-order rather than waiting until the release date. You can do this by giving value right away—for example, you can send a bonus ebook, add readers to a special email list, or give them an early-bird version of the book.

❯ Make sure to tap the ecosystem around pre-order tactics, such as using ARC services for securing reviews or submitting your title for a BookBub new release feature.

Resources

> All about Pre-Orders:
> http://authornews.penguinrandomhouse.com/all-about-pre-orders/

> The 13 Pre-Order Strategies That Increase Book Sales:
> https://www.amarketingexpert.com/the-13-pre-order-strategies-that-increase-book-sales/

> How I Promoted a Preorder to Launch a Bestselling Book:
> https://insights.bookbub.com/promoted-preorder-launch-bestselling-book/

TACTIC 13

AMAZON BESTSELLER BADGE TACTIC

Description

Did you know that even though the "bestseller" label has been overused, it is still an instant credibility booster for authors and books? Why is that?

Let us admit that people use the word "bestseller" too freely. Also, Amazon's ranking algorithms and multiple Bestseller lists have created numerous "bestselling" authors. But the fact remains that most people who are not in the book selling world have no idea how this label gets applied, so they see "bestseller" status simply as a badge of success. That why "landing a bestseller" is still a superb tactic—it increases your credibility and your book's.

Now I am not advocating applying this label loosely and irrespective of your book's actual success. You still need to use it appropriately, which means writing a solid book and promoting it in the relevant categories. But used correctly on Amazon, the bestseller tactic can be a powerful one.

Amazon is still the best retailer for achieving bestseller status. The smartest approach is to enroll in Amazon's KDP Select program and reserve a free promotion period of up to 5 days. Alternatively, you can target paid lists by going for a Countdown deal. Landing a bestseller this way is more difficult, but on the other hand, you can not only make a campaign profitable but also increase your ranking on Amazon much more sustainably than with a free promotion. During the Amazon promotion time you book 1–3 promotions with discounted ebook alert services, such as BookGorilla, Booksends, or Freebooksy. Be sure to monitor the Kindle bestseller list for free (or paid) books in your categories every couple of hours during your promotion days. If you follow these steps, you have a particularly good chance of landing a bestseller.

Examples of Success

Example: Chris Fox

Learn directly from author Chris Fox how he launched an Amazon Bestseller in 2017.

Thumbnail (February 10, 2020): YouTube, Chris Fox: How I Launched an Amazon Bestseller, https://www.youtube.com/watch?v=GJqom_fIVtE

Application

> Enroll in Amazon's KDP Select program and reserve a free book promotion or a Countdown deal period lasting up to 5 days. During that time book 1–3 promotions with discounted ebook alert services, such as BookGorilla, Booksends, or Freebooksy.

> Be sure to monitor the Kindle bestseller list for free or paid books in your categories every couple of hours during your promotion days.

> To get the most out of this tactic, submit up to 10 categories directly to Amazon Support (including

some categories that aren't super competitive but still relevant to your book; see the tutorial in "Resources") in order to increase your chances of reaching bestseller status by ranking high on less competitive lists.

Resources

> Book Marketing 101: How to Hit #1 on Amazon's Bestseller List:
> https://okdork.com/hit-1-amazons-bestseller-list/

> How to Add More Amazon Book Categories to Your Book:
> https://www.youtube.com/watch?v=2GO-XNAoepE

> How to Get Amazon Bestseller Badge:
> https://www.youtube.com/watch?v=WaFkPd_J_Ss

> How to Land the Amazon Bestseller List in Your Niche:
> https://mcdium.com/better-marketing/how-to-land-the-amazon-bestseller-list-in-your-niche-4a838b19e9ae

TACTIC 14

PINTEREST TRAFFIC GENERATION

Description

Pinterest boasts an astounding 250 million users a month. For marketers, an even more interesting statistic is that 90 percent of these users frequent the platform to make purchase decisions, and 55 percent of Pinners are specifically searching for products.[1] So not only is Pinterest a great channel for reaching your target audience, but it is also ripe for attracting buyers. Even better, Pinterest allows you to create a pin related to your book, which will drive traffic to your personal website or Amazon page.

But there is an even smarter way to market your books through Pinterest. When you use Pinterest in combination with a third-party service called Tailwind Tribes, you can team up with other authors and content creators in your niche who have a comparable number of followers to cross-promote each other's content. I will share more in the "Application" section. Tactic 14 is about turbocharging your book selling through the synergy of these two powerful tools.

---

1   https://blog.hootsuite.com/pinterest-statistics-for-business/.

Examples of Success

Example: Brit Poe

Adult Fantasy author Brit Poe's channel is getting 170K viewers per month by leveraging Pinterest and Tailwind Tribes.

Thumbnail (February 5, 2020): https://www.pinterest.co.uk/britpoeandco/

Example: Susan Earlham

Novelist Susan Earlham's pins get 65K viewers monthly.

Thumbnail (February 5, 2020): https://www.pinterest.co.uk/susanlearlam/

Example: Jenn Beach PA

Jenn Beach PA manages to get more than 15K viewers to her pins every month.

Thumbnail (February 5, 2020): https://www.pinterest.com/jennbeachpa/

Application

> First, set up your Pinterest business account (not a personal account) on business.pinterest.com. The business account gives you access to precious analytics on repins, clicks, and views. Fill out your profile and include your book funnel.

> Next, showcase your personality and build your author identity by creating engaging boards. Create lots of boards on the subtopics within your niche. For instance, you could create boards for all the books you have written and are going to write, for your favorite authors, and for the top 10 books you've read this year. Pin 10–20 images per board. Use relevant keywords for your niche and brand, and make sure the pins are relevant too. Images should be high-quality, descriptions should be engaging, and your pinning should be consistent and regular. However, keep in mind that you do not want to overwhelm your audience with too many pins.

> Create pins for your own content and add a watermark. Create a Pinterest-sized image (W: 1,000 px; H: 1,500 px) for each post that you want to promote to your site from Pinterest. Canva.com and other free programs offer an easy way to create images. When your pins are ready, upload them and target the relevant post on your website. Upload each of your pins to a separate board.

> If you are thinking of using Tailwind Tribes, first sign up for the free trial version. This gives you access to 5 Tribes and 30 shares per month, so you can learn the ropes and see if you want to invest in a paid

subscription. A paid membership costs $7.50 per month and gives you Tribes PowerUps, boosting your exposure.

> To get started on Tailwind, fill out your profile and link to your Pinterest account. To become a member of a Tribe, click the "Tribes" feature and identify your Tribe (i.e., your niche). Use "Find a Tribe" to search for more Tribes; select one that looks like a good fit and request to join. Once accepted, you will be able to nominate which of the Tribe's content you want to share. It is reciprocal: the more you share, the more they'll share of yours. To use Tailwind effectively, aim to post 30–50 pins per day. That sounds like a lot, but Tailwind makes it easy by giving you the option to post your pins days, weeks, or even months in advance.

> Finally, to get the most out of Tailwind, you will want to track and measure. Measure the number of reins, reshapes, and pieces of content you have shared. Double down on the high-performing Tribes, and do not be afraid to leave (or stop contributing to) Tribes that are not performing. Ideally, you will want to post 50% your own content and 50% from other pinners.

Resources

> How to Skyrocket your Pinterest Traffic with Tailwind Tribes:
> https://www.youtube.com/
> watch?v=B6pJgGNxe_g&feature=emb_title

> How to Get Traffic To Your Website (Fast!) 2019:
> https://www.youtube.com/watch?v=Vi1RyAN8nFw

> Tailwind Tribes: A Step-by-Step Guide to Exploding Your Pinterest Traffic Fast:
> https://conversionminded.com/tailwind-tribes/

> Pinterest for Authors:
> https://jennbeachpa.com/2018/02/13/pinterest-for-authors/

TACTIC 15

BUILDING AN AUTHOR PLATFORM WITH EMAIL MARKETING

Description

Authors sometimes think that email marketing as a tactic for platform building has gone the way of the dinosaurs—if it is not already extinct, it will be soon. Nothing could be further from the truth.

Yes, email marketing has become a highly competitive, super crowded arena. But done right, it can be a tremendous way of building your platform. How do you do that? By focusing on building a platform of engaged subscribers. The rule here is that it is better to have 1,000 dedicated fans than 10,000 casual subscribers with low open rates and little interaction.

When you are building your platform with email marketing, start small and think personally. It is easy to feel intimidated by the big-name influencers and brand-name authors who have upward of 10,000 subscribers, but do not be. Getting to your first 1,000 dedicated subscribers—even to your first 100—is already a huge achievement. It is a mark many authors and marketers don't hit.

Simply put, platform building with an email list of true fans is still one of the best author tactics for 2020 and beyond.

Examples of Success

Example: Derek Murphy

Derek Murphy was able to get 8,500+ new readers on his email list BEFORE publishing his first book with giveaways.

Learn more about how he did it by visiting https://www.creativindie.com/how-to-use-kingsumo-and-rafflecopter-to-build-your-email-list-likes-and-follows-quickly-with-giveaways/.

Thumbnail (February 10, 2020): Created on PicsSee

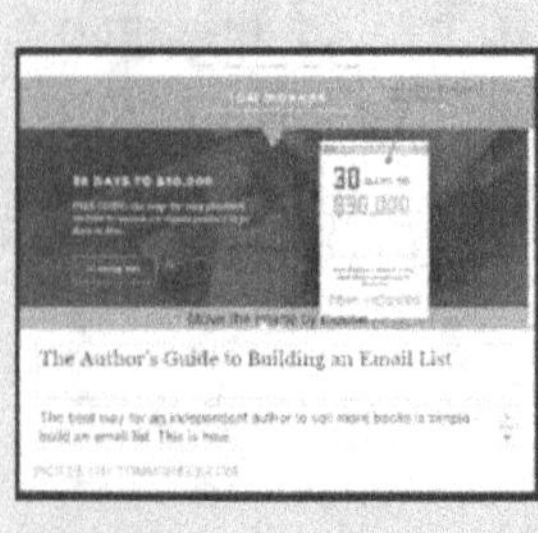

Example: Tom Morkes

Author Tom Morkes shares how he was able to build an impressive email list that helped him make sales from his books.

Learn more about how he did it by visiting https://tommorkes.com/author-email-list/.

Thumbnail (February 10, 2020): Created on PicsSee

Application

> Focus on building an author platform where you have engaged, loyal fans (ideally as email subscribers) as opposed to occasional or casual fans.

> Remember, it is more valuable to have 100–1,000 true connections, subscribers who you know personally, than 1,000–10,000 subscribers who are barely involved and where you struggle with open rates.

> Invest in an email marketing software and set up an autoresponder.

> Use viral marketing tactics like giveaways and challenges to grow your fan base more quickly and pass 1,000 subscribers.

Resources

> How to Build an Author Platform: Free Course: https://www.ingramspark.com/author-platform-course-description

> Q&A: ESTABLISHING YOUR AUTHOR PLATFORM: https://www.authorsguild.org/whats-new/seminars-member-events/business-webinars-writers/qa-establishing-author-platform/

> 0 to 1000 Email Subscribers in 30 Days: How to Grow Your Email List Fast: https://www.youtube.com/watch?v=UNvGIch-u74

TACTIC 16

COLLABORATIVE BOOK PROMOTION

Description

Being an author can feel a bit lonely sometimes, especially when it comes to book marketing. We are often fighting alone for book sales, publicity, shares, and mentions. Wouldn't it be great if we could team up with somebody? That is where Tactic 16 comes in.

Two factors make the tactic of collaborative book promotions effective:

(1) Reaching a wider, more relevant audience more quickly; and

(2) Getting recommended by a voice that people trust. Number 2 is especially important, because recommendations count heavily for authors, just like reviews.

This tactic is about tapping into the power of recommendations by engaging in various forms of collaborative book promotion, such as newsletter swaps, joint giveaways, and cross-promotion on social media.

Examples of Success

Example: JJ Toner

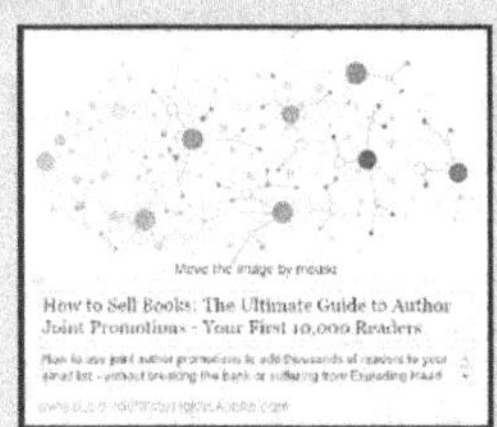

Irish novelist JJ Toner describes how a carefully orchestrated collaboration between indie authors of books about the Second World War truly engaged readers, with marketing benefits for all involved. The campaign helped sell 542 copies of his own book on pre-order.

Learn more about how he did it by visiting https://selfpublishingadvice.org/jj-toner-author-collaboration/.

Thumbnail (February 10, 2020): Created on PicsSee

Example: Nick Stephenson

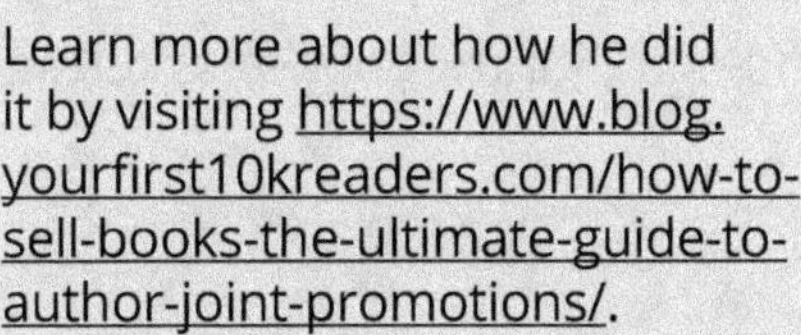

Nick Stephenson shares many examples of successful joint promotions, among them his Mystery / Thriller boxed set. He teamed up with 7 other authors to put together an anthology of short stories called Eight the Hard Way. With more than 50,000 downloads and hundreds of great reviews, this book is still getting hundreds of downloads every week, years since its release.

Learn more about how he did it by visiting https://www.blog.yourfirst10kreaders.com/how-to-sell-books-the-ultimate-guide-to-author-joint-promotions/.

Thumbnail (February 10, 2020): Created on PicsSee

Application

> Reach out to other authors in your genre to cross-promote via email (i.e., newsletter swaps) and social media.

> Boost each other's publicity by guest blogging and making guest appearances on each other's YouTube channels.

> Organize a joint giveaway to benefit each author's audience and gain exposure to a new crowd.

> Create boxed sets.

Resources

> 13 AUTHORS' STORIES: THE ULTIMATE GUIDE TO JOINT PROMOTIONS: https://www.blog.yourfirst10kreaders.com/how-to-sell-books-the-ultimate-guide-to-author-joint-promotions/

> How to Promote Your Book with Newsletter Swaps: https://www.youtube.com/watch?v=-pKnhZc9VCI

> 10 WAYS AUTHORS COLLABORATE TO PROMOTE THEIR BOOKS: https://theempoweredauthor.com/lounge-blog/how-authors-collaborate-book-marketing

TACTIC 17

VIDEO MARKETING ON YOUTUBE, AMAZON & BEYOND

Description

As authors, our medium is text, but we cannot ignore the massive influence of video on consumers' experience today. Consider these statistics:[2]

> By 2021, 82% of all internet traffic will be video traffic.

> 96% of consumers watch explainer videos to learn more about products and services.

> Adding a video to a landing page can increase conversion by as much as 80%.

> YouTube is the second largest search engine in the world, with a whopping 2 billion logged-in users per month.

> 70% of what YouTubers watch is determined by the platform's recommendation algorithm.

In other words, video is huge. Authors who embrace video to reach their audience have a big advantage in the marketplace, as many have already demonstrated by running popular YouTube channels. In the end we are all

---

2   See   https://www.techsmith.com/blog/increase-conversion-rates-video/;   https://www.searchenginejournal.com/seo-101/meet-search-engines/;   and   https://blog.hootsuite.com/youtube-stats-marketers/.

storytellers, and video is a phenomenal means of telling a story.

Tactic 17 shows you how to use video through your website, Amazon account, or YouTube channel to powerfully tell your story, grow your audience, and increase conversion rates.

Examples of Success

Kristen Martin, Joanna Penn, and Jeff Goins are examples of authors leveraging YouTube to promote their books—with great success. Check out their YouTube channels for inspiration on how to build your own.

Example: Kristen Martin

Thumbnail (February 20, 2020): https://www.youtube.com/channel/UCYyy_hiZRaSLGLOn62Nc4AA

Example: Joanna Penn

Thumbnail (February 20, 2020): https://www.youtube.com/user/thecreativepenn

Example: Jeff Goins

Thumbnail (February 20, 2020): https://www.youtube.com/channel/UCXsSdIE-hbv-BwP1epYWzXg

Another great strategy for authors and publishers is to promote their books through video shorts on Amazon. See the examples below.[3]

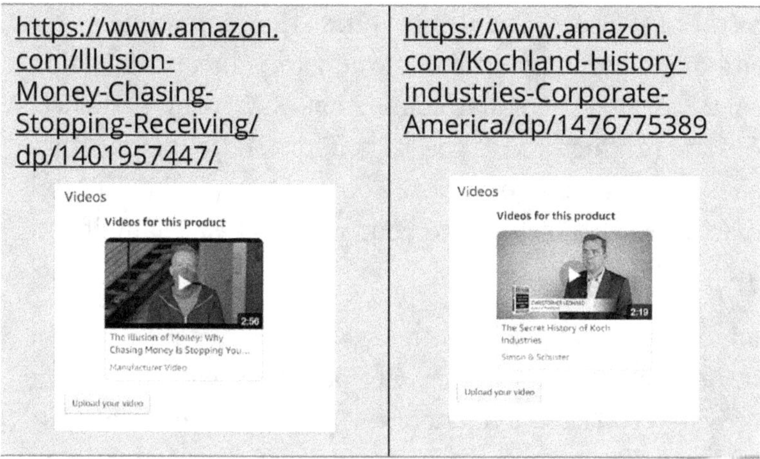

https://www.amazon. com/Illusion-Money-Chasing-Stopping-Receiving/ dp/1401957447/	https://www.amazon. com/Kochland-History-Industries-Corporate-America/dp/1476775389

You can also use video on Amazon Author Central to show your audience that you have authority by sharing interviews or sequences of training sessions, as author Patrick McKeown does (see the screenshot below).

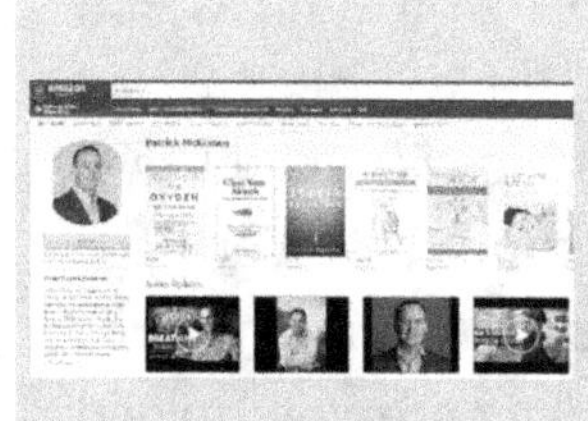

Example: Patrick McKeown

Thumbnail (February 20, 2020): https://www.amazon. com/Patrick-McKeown/e/ B006X1OD3U?ref=sr_ntt_srch_ lnk_1&qid=1580733651&sr=8-1

---

3 Note: Brand Registry is required at the time of writing, but I suspect KDP will soon allow authors to upload videos to their sales pages.

Application

Follow the lead of the authors above by creating videos for your own YouTube channel, Amazon page, or Author Central account. Video multiplies the possibilities for communication. You can tell your story in an appealing format, make a personal connection with your audience, promote products and special offers, share behind-the-scenes information (e.g., why you wrote your book), and impart special knowledge to your viewers (especially if you write nonfiction).

Many people hate seeing themselves on camera or feel awkward talking to a device. Get past that fear by starting a private YouTube channel so only you can see your performance! Record a short video of yourself talking about a random topic every day or once a week. Keep it simple, and don't worry about whether it's great. Upload it to your channel. As you do this regularly, you'll get faster, more polished, and more confident in front of the camera.

There are a few things to keep in mind if you want to put time and energy into YouTube. First, do a little market research and plan a long-term strategy. Video is competitive, and you want to be seen. Second, remember that YouTube is a search engine—that means optimizing your keywords to show up in search results. Third, make sure you upload high-quality videos in good lighting. Your phone camera is probably sufficient for your YouTube needs, but you will want to buy a microphone for better audio.

Finally, do not overthink it, and do not worry about perfection! If you put it off, you will never get to it. Just try to strike a balance between spontaneity and preparedness on camera so you come across as confident, natural, and relaxed.

Resources

> 10 Tips for Starting a YouTube Channel: https://www.adorama.com/alc/10-tips-for-starting-a-youtube-channel

> Promote Your Book with Video — Author Marketing Tips: https://www.youtube.com/watch?v=B-NwMnZxnfM

> 4 Strategies of Video Marketing for Self-Published Books: https://www.youtube.com/watch?v=U1aXDBcAP7k

> How To Use Video Marketing Like A Hollywood Director: https://www.thecreativepenn.com/2018/04/20/video-marketing/

> An Epic Guide to YouTube Video Marketing for Authors: https://booklaunchers.com/youtube-video-marketing-authors/

TACTIC 18

AMAZON SELECT PRICE PROMO + DISCOUNTED BOOK SERVICE

Description

Tactic 18 might not sound very cutting-edge if you are an experienced book marketer in 2020. However, although it is true that results today aren't quite what they were in 2013, 2014, or 2015, this tactic is still a great way of getting attention at an affordable price.

The concept is simple: You use discounted ebook alert services with a price promotion through Amazon KDP Select. See the Application section of this chapter for details.

Depending on the scale of the promotion (based on audience size and quality of the third-party service), you can easily reach 100,000 targeted readers, getting hundreds or thousands of downloads for a free book and sales for a discounted book.

This tactic can jumpstart your book sales, bring you bestseller status (as shown in a different tactic), but most importantly, boost your audience. That's why it's vital to have marketing systems—like email signup on your webpage—already in place and to ensure that your book is error-free and already has some reviews. If you have not created a way of connecting with your readers down the line, a "cold promotion" can backfire in the form of bad reviews or a wasted effort.

Examples of Success

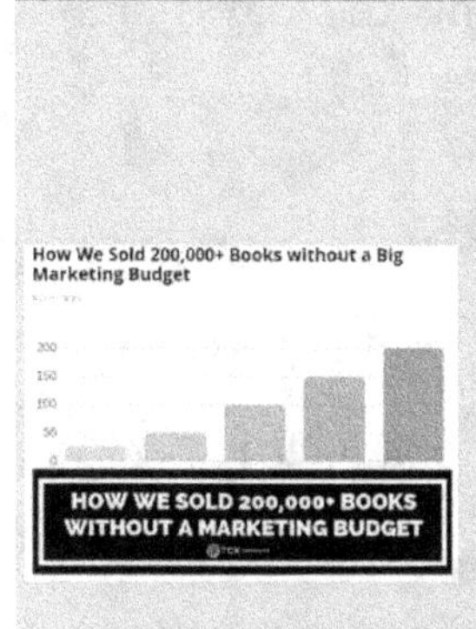

Example: Tom Corson

Tom Corson Knowles shares how his team managed to share 200,000+ copies of *Unlimited Memory*, by Kevin Horsley, through KDP Select and featured deals on BookBub. (Note: Sales started in 2014. This strategy isn't quite as dynamic today.)

Thumbnail (February 10, 2020): https://www.tckpublishing.com/how-we-sold-200000-books-without-a-marketing-budget/

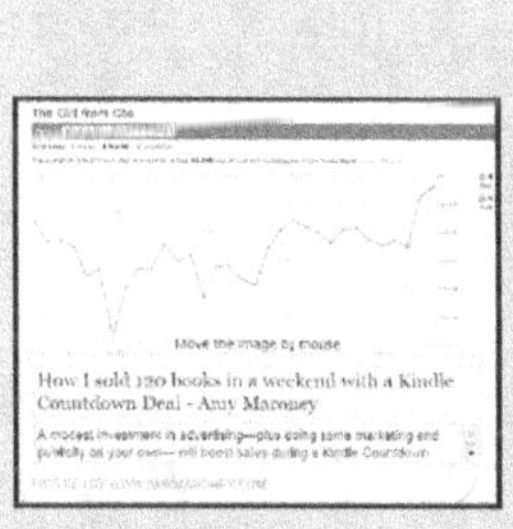

Example: Amy Maroney

Author Amy Maroney sold 120 books in a single weekend with a Kindle Countdown Deal.

Learn more about how she did it by visiting:

https://www.amymaroney.com/2017/02/25/how-i-sold-120-books-in-a-weekend-with-a-kindle-countdown-deal/.

Thumbnail (February 10, 2020): Created on PicsSee

Application

> Enroll your book in KDP Select. Make sure it's available exclusively on Amazon and nowhere else.

> Choose a price promotion (either free or countdown deal).

> Secure promotions with third-party discounted ebook alert services (list of services) during the days your book is on promo on Amazon.

Resources

> Kindle Countdown Deals:
> https://kdp.amazon.com/en_US/help/topic/G201293780

> Free Book Promotions:
> https://kdp.amazon.com/en_US/help/topic/G201298240

> KDP Select and BookBub Promotions: An Indie Author Experience:
> https://theseatedview.com/2019/03/kdp-select-and-bookbub-promotions-an-indie-author-experience.html

> How to Use KDP Countdown Deals — Kindle Publishing in 2020:
> https://www.youtube.com/watch?v=SmXRfqRAMEA

TACTIC 19

AUTHORITY BOOK PUBLISHING

Description

"Authority Book Publishing" is not directly about increasing sales. This unique tactic has to do with establishing credibility and influence and helping you reach higher-level business or career goals. Rather than merely aiming at more sales—something every author wants—you will be aiming to show your expertise in a way that enhances your image and ultimately your career.

Having a goal like this can help you straighten out your priorities and save you a lot of headache in terms of publishing and sales. Your focus will be on launching a strong book with solid content, which will appear on your webpage or social media profiles in ways that add value for readers. You might even distribute it for free in your business marketing activities.

What makes this tactic so powerful? It is that we as humans are born to follow leaders. We are conditioned to recognize authorities and pay attention to what they have to say, whether they are doctors, scholars, employers, or others in a position of superior knowledge and influence. Authors belong in that category too. Being an author still carries weight in our society. It shows that you have insight, that you are qualified to speak on a certain subject.

So, find your niche—the area where you have something special or unique to offer—and start writing. If you are still doubtful that your skills or knowledge can make you a successful author, take this little test: Would you rather buy a service from a business owner who has published a book on their industry area or one who has not? Who you go with the first? Do not underestimate the power of writing a book to establish authority!

Examples of Success

Example: Brianna Ruelas

Brianna Ruelas had no idea what to write about. But when she wrote a book about her area of expertise—navigating the music industry—she started raking in $4,000 per month from new clients who came to her for career consulting.

Learn more about how she did it by visiting:

https://self-publishingschool. com/from-no-book-idea-to-4000- per-month/.

Thumbnail (February 10, 2020): Created on PicsSee

How Russell Brunson Built A $100 Million
Company & Mass Movement With ClickFunnels

FREE VIRTUAL TRAINING EVENT WITH TONY ROBBINS, DEAN

Example: Russell Brunson

Successful entrepreneur Russell Brunson hit gold when he started the company ClickFunnels. What some people don't know is that his books played a huge part in this journey.

Learn more by watching https://www.youtube.com/watch?v=oqylAaNkFhA.

Thumbnail (February 10, 2020): Created on PicsSee

Example: Rob Moore

Rob Moore, an expert on property investing, built the training company Progressive Success. He's also one of the UK's leading nonfiction authors. His books feed directly into his business by attracting readers to his free weekend workshops, where, after having already invested time reading his £10 book and attended his seminar, they're more likely to commit to one of his £2,000 courses.

Find out more at https://robmoore.com/books/.

Thumbnail (February 10, 2020): Created on PicsSee

Application

Remember, this tactic is not about making quick money but about proving yourself an authority in a specific niche to "qualify leads" (i.e., attract likely customers)—leads who will buy more from you at a later stage. You invest in building your credibility now so that it pays off down the road.

At this point, you need to consider what it is you will be offering people in the end. What is your most expensive package? Personal consulting? An online course? Now, work backwards from that point. Think of the journey you're taking your audience on and map it out in reverse: start with your most valuable offer and trace your way back to your initial offering—your book.

In real time, you are going to present the book to prospective buyers (a micro-commitment on their part) and then gradually lead them to more and more expensive offers (bigger commitments). It must be a gradual process; that is the only way it will work. Imagine if we had just met and I asked you for a million dollars. You would laugh and say I was crazy. Or imagine asking someone to marry you on the first date—they would probably walk away. Similarly, you need to earn your readers' trust and commitment over time. Start with a small offer and then lead them to the more valuable offers.

That is how it works. Now you can get to writing! In Book Marketing Secrets, I talk about how your book is the star. You want to write a quality book, something people will enjoy reading and get value from. Writing can be a challenging process, but if you have built up expertise in your field, it will be much easier. You will be speaking from what you know. If you do not already have the knowledge to write a book on your subject, it is time to start learning.

Finally, some practical pointers: Your book will sit at the beginning of your book funnel at a low price, or even for free. Pitch it to people who are likely to be interested using Google ads, Facebook ads, SEO, podcasts, blogs, etc. The book funnel will act as a tripwire to qualify your leads. They are "qualified" because they've shown interest by clicking on the download button or, if the book costs something, by pulling out their credit card to purchase.

As a rule of thumb, out of a thousand people who view the book, fifty will buy. By the time those fifty have finished reading your book, you will have convinced them that you know what you are talking about. They have started to trust you, and they are now more likely to buy your more expensive offers.

Resources

> How to Write a Book to Grow Your Business:
> https://self-publishingschool.com/write-a-book-about-your-business/

> Do I Need a Book for My Business?:
> http://blog.raybrehm.com/do-i-need-a-book-for-my-business/

> 45 Marketing Experts Share Their Authority Building Strategies:
> https://www.authoritycontent.com/marketing/how-to-become-an-expert/

> Here's What Every Entrepreneur Should Know about Becoming an Author:
> https://www.forbes.com/sites/bryancollinseurope/2019/06/20/heres-what-every-entrepreneur-should-know-about-becoming-an-author

TACTIC 20

SIMPLE BUT POWERFUL AMAZON SEO

Description

Search engine optimization, or SEO, is not something we authors normally think about when publishing and marketing books. However, it is one of the most important skills an online marketer can have. SEO is critical for high keyword rankings and subsequent visibility of books online.

SEO is a vast subject, certainly too big to cover in depth in a book like this one, but I have distilled it into a basic blueprint that I share in this chapter.

Tactic 20 gives you three concrete steps for doing effective SEO on Amazon: (1) using 1–3 main keywords that have solid research volume, (2) adding those keywords to the title/subtitle/description, and (3) monitoring rankings over time to take further action.

The game plan in this chapter is simple enough for anyone to follow. It leaves out the more intricate SEO tools in the domain of pro marketers but still gives you a handle on top SEO activities.

Examples of Success

The following examples demonstrate just how big a difference good SEO can make in a book's prospects of showing up in search results. Clearly, it is important to include main keywords in the title and subtitle. By using even one keyword with search volume in your title, you already ensure success for your book due to organic traffic.

1. Results for the keywords "Oxygen" (left) and "Keto Diet" (right). It is worth noting that a novel appears in the first 10 results for "Oxygen," a highly search keyword, and the top two results for "Keto Diet" have "Keto Diet" as the first words in the title.

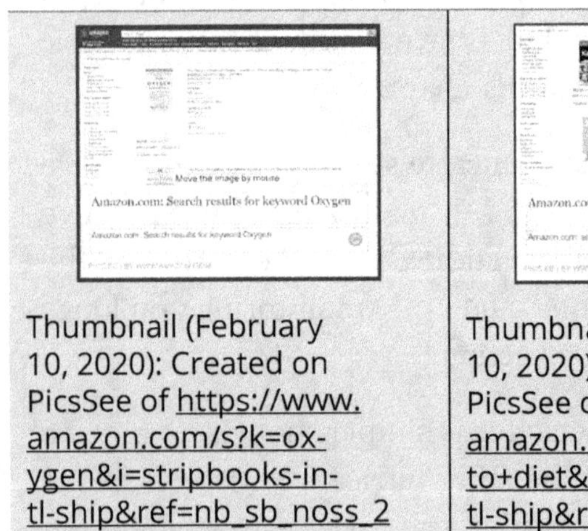

Thumbnail (February 10, 2020): Created on PicsSee of https://www.amazon.com/s?k=oxygen&i=stripbooks-intl-ship&ref=nb_sb_noss_2

Thumbnail (February 10, 2020): Created on PicsSee of https://www.amazon.com/s?k=keto+diet&i=stripbooks-intl-ship&ref=nb_sb_noss_2

2. Results for the keyword "self-publishing." There are many good books on self-publishing, but if you enter it as a keyword, you will only get results that use this word in the title.

Thumbnail (February 10, 2020): Created on PicsSee of https://www.amazon.com/s?k=self-publishing&ref=nb_sb_noss_2

Application

> Use 1-3 keywords that have good search volume. Use the Google Keyword Tool and the Chrome Browser Extension of Keywords Everywhere (or the paid version of keywordtool.io) to get free information on search volume on Amazon and Google. Alternatively, you can use the paid product KDP Rocket, which also gives you estimates of Amazon search volume.

> Add those keywords to your title/subtitle/description. Title is, of course, the biggest ranking factor, followed by subtitle and then description. If you use Amazon KDP, make sure to also include your most relevant search terms in KDP's backend keywords/search terms. Please also note that each book format has a separate landing page, so make sure to fill out both and to use little variations to increase your reach.

> Monitor your book's rankings over time and take further action. Use egrow.io (free plan) to follow your rankings. Egrow allows you to monitor up to 5 keywords for free, so you can see if you rank. If your book is not showing up in searches, try using less competitive keywords.

Resources

> Amazon Ranking Hacks:
> https://startupbros.com/amazon-ranking-hacks/

> 21 Ways to Rank Your Products Higher on Amazon:
> https://www.repricerexpress.com/rank-your-products-higher-on-amazon/

> Get up to 10 Amazon Categories for Your Book:
> https://www.youtube.com/watch?v=2GO-XNAoepE

TACTIC 21

RUNNING AMAZON AMS ADS

Description

There are a few features that set apart Amazon Marketing Services (AMS) ads and make them superior to other advertising channels, such as Facebook, Google, or smaller ad promotions:

> They appear directly at the point of sale, targeting users with buy intent.

> They offer very transparent and simple data, making it easy for authors to assess profitability.

> They are easy to set up and less risky than, for instance, Facebook ads.

Examples of Success

Two Reedsy Case Studies (both from 2017): https://blog.reedsy.com/amazon-ads-for-authors-case-studies/

Application

> Set up a simple AMS ad campaign (sponsored product) with automated targeting, with a low daily budget.

> Set up a simple AMS ad campaign (sponsored product) with manual targeting, going for keywords and book categories.

> Check results on an ongoing basis. Assess your real profitability by only calculating your royalties (net profit) instead of total sales.

> If you run keyword-driven campaigns, remove the keywords that are not performing over time and work on individual cost-per-click (CPC) prices for each keyword based on its performance.

Resources

> How to Double Your Book Sales with AMS Ads: https://www.youtube.com/watch?v=5TSj-GiGd2M

> Free Course for AMS ads by Kindlepreneur: https://kindlepreneur.com/ams-book-advertising-course/

> How to Find 1000's of Profitable Keywords for Your Amazon Ads in Less Than 10 Minutes: https://www.youtube.com/watch?v=b4psDxMFjbc

> Amazon Marketing Services: 20 Creative & Unique Ways to Use AMS Ads: https://self-publishingschool.com/amazon-marketing-services/

TACTIC 22

AUDIOBOOK CREATION AND AUDIOBOOK GIVEAWAYS

Description

Audiobooks are the fastest-growing content medium for publishers today. While many publishers have jumped on the bandwagon, the ratio of books (including ebooks) to audiobooks for most subjects—e.g., the Keto Diet on Amazon—is still only about 20 to 1. So, while audiobooks are a hot market, there's still truly little competition in some categories. It is a prime field for enterprising authors and publishers to get in on.

While I highly recommend publishing audiobooks, it is equally important to promote them using the right tactics. That is why this chapter deals with running Audiobook Giveaways through Audiobook Boom and garncring reviews by using dedicated services.[4]

---

4   See www.audiobookboom.com/authors and https://katetilton. com/25-ways-market-audiobook-quick-guide/.

Examples of Success

Example: Ashton Cartwright

Ashton Cartwright of Paidauthor shared his results using Audiobook promo codes and giveaways for one of his biggest clients in the contemporary romance/erotica genre in 2019 on his website. His efforts resulted in around $6,000 in extra royalties.

Thumbnail (February 10, 2020): https://youtu.be/WMhU3bWf-YI

Example: Wiley Brooks

Author Wiley Brooks ran a promotion with Audiobook Boom (January 1, 2020) and secured 3+ fresh reviews on Audible within the next 28 days.

Thumbnail (February 10, 2020): https://www.paidauthor.com/audible-or-acx-codes-and-where-to-give-them-away/

Thumbnail: Audiobook Boom Newsletter, https://mailchi.mp/audiobookboom/your-free-audiobook-boom-for-123119

Thumbnail: Audible Audiobook page, https://www.audible.com/pd/The-Next-Best-Thing-Audiobook/B0831CL9M4

Application

> Make your book available as an audiobook. I recommend using Amazon's Audiobook Creation Exchange (ACX) or Findaway Voices.

> When you publish, think "audiobook first." Do not just pass on a print/ebook manuscript to a narrator—adapt the original text or create a dedicated manuscript for an audio version.

> Get promo codes from ACX (25 in the US, 25 in the UK) or Findaway Voices (100 with Voices Plus) and run audiobook giveaways through sites like audiobookboom.com, which will share your giveaway with as many as 10K people. If you're especially tech-savvy, you can also organize your own giveaway on Facebook using Gleam.io.[5] Currently Audible even pays royalties when readers listen to your audiobook by redeeming a free code—an amazing deal!

> Get reviews by making your audiobook accessible through dedicated audiobook review submission services.

> Submit your audiobook for consideration as part of a featured deal on Chirp Books (run by Bookbub). See www.chirpbooks.com.

---

5 How to Run a Viral Giveaway on Facebook: https://www. youtube.com/watch?v=5tJDt5yw-z4

Resources

> 25 Ways to Market Your Audiobook: A Quick Guide: https://katetilton.com/25-ways-market-audiobook-quick-guide/

> How to Market an Audiobook: https://www.thecreativepenn.com/how-to-market-an-audiobook/

> Audible or ACX Codes and Where to Give Them Away: https://www.paidauthor.com/audible-or-acx-codes-and-where-to-give-them-away/

> Get Cookin' with New and Improved Promo Codes: https://blog.acx.com/2019/05/09/get-cookin-with-new-and-improved-promo-codes/

TACTIC 23

RETARGETING WITH FACEBOOK ADVERTISING + MESSENGER MARKETING

Description

Facebook ads have been a favorite tool of online marketers for years. Their great advantage lies in their ability to target users very specifically. However, please do not read Tactic 23 as an all-out recommendation to run Facebook ads. Without some marketing savvy, newbies can do more damage than good and end up wasting a lot of money.

Still, there are two powerful Facebook advertising tactics that I do recommend based on the results they have had for my clients. One is Facebook retargeting. The other is Facebook Messenger marketing.

To understand retargeting, it helps to realize that there are three basic types of audiences: cold, warm, and hot. Cold audiences are those seeing your content for the first time. They do not know you, do not know if they can trust you, and will not buy from you without further proof. They are still in evaluation mode. Hot audiences, on the other hand, are those who have seen your ads, purchased your products, and know your brand. They are committed.

If you are starting out as a Facebook marketer, the people you want to target (or retarget) are "warm": they are already aware of your existence and just need to be brought in. The reality is that your target readers need to see your offer—i.e., your book—many times before they will purchase.

So how do you retarget a warm audience? Fortunately, Facebook allows you to send ads to users who have previously interacted with your content in some way, even if they haven't shared their information. You can do this by installing a Facebook Pixel, an embedded code in your funnel that lets you retarget anyone who visited your website.

The second part of this tactic is using Facebook Messenger as a strategic marketing tool. Marketing on Messenger yields 10–80 times better engagement than email marketing, reporting astonishing 88% open rates and 56% clickthrough rates for certain campaigns. Facebook Messenger marketing is still new terrain, but if you can get in on it with a smart campaign (see examples below) and set up simple autoresponders through ManyChat.

Examples of Success

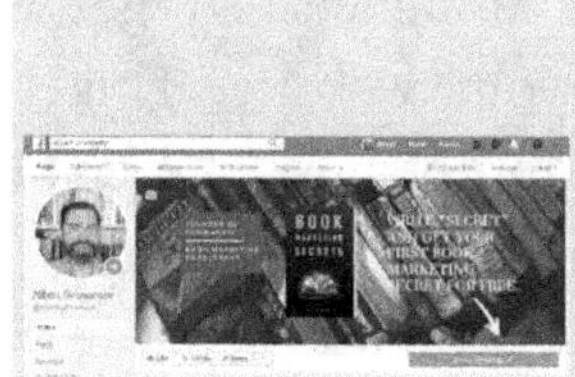

Example: Albert Griesmayr

I use my Facebook page as a hub for Messenger marketing. Visitors get a reward for connecting via Messenger (i.e., by sending a message), and responses are automated through ManyChat.

Example: Chandler Bolt

Chandler Bolt of Self Publishing School demonstrates how to retarget ads, directly addressing audiences in a way that shows they've previously visited his webpage.

Thumbnail (February 3, 2020): https://www.facebook.com/ads/library/?active_status=all&ad_type=all&country=AT&impression_search_field=has_impressions_lifetime&view_all_page_id=751114201604736

Application

> Collect data for creating a warm audience. To get started, install Facebook Pixel on your website. This is a lot easier than it sounds; you do not need a tech background or any IT experience at all. YouTube and Facebook make it simple for you to create and activate the Pixel, which will track visitors and collect essential information for building an audience profile. Once you understand who is viewing your content, you can design retargeting campaigns aimed at those users or "Lookalike Audiences."

> Learn more about Facebook Messenger marketing and ManyChat. Brainstorm creative ways to boost your audience outreach with these tools.

> There are two types of ads to be aware of: (1) Video ads are great for talking to your readers about a new book or about your writing process. You can create them simply, with minimal equipment and no professional crew required. (See also the YouTube tactic for more information.) (2) Carousel ads feature multiple images for viewers to swipe through. You might want to showcase artwork from inside your book, or maybe you are looking to promote multiple books in a single ad. You can also make each image in the sequence a different type of ad.

> The main thing is to find what works for your genre and your specific kind of readers. Always think from the reader's perspective!

Resources

> Facebook Retargeting Ads: A Step-by-Step Guide to Sending Website Visitors on a Facebook Retargeting Journey: https://www.abetterlemonadestand.com/facebook-retargeting-ads/

> What's Working Right Now: Facebook Ads: https://selfpublishingformula.com/episode-175/

> Create and Install a Facebook Pixel: https://www.facebook.com/business/help/952192354843755?id=1205376682832142

> Facebook Messenger Chatbot Marketing: The Definitive Guide (Updated for 2020): https://www.crowdspring.com/blog/facebook-messenger-marketing-guide/

TACTIC 24

KOBO PUBLISHING

Description

Tactic 24 is a bit out-of-the-box, and that is a good thing. Since the market is so competitive, sometimes it is smart not to copy what everyone else is doing.

We all know that Amazon towers over the industry with its insanely large market share, but other retailers—like Barnes & Noble, Apple Books, and Kobo—have big audiences too. If you can dominate keywords or categories on those platforms, you can generate healthy sales there as well. In this chapter I'm focusing on the opportunity for authors on Kobo.

The Kobo Publishing Tactic can be quite beneficial for authors who aren't exclusively enrolled in KDP Select and are looking to run promotions with less competition. At the time of writing, Kobo has special promotions for books in the Romance, Science Fiction, and Mysteries & Thrillers departments.

Examples of Success

The screenshot below (circle added) gives you an overview of the different promotions you can run on Kobo. If you publish directly through the service, you have access to Kobo Promotions. It is possible you might have to contact Support to get it (as I did), but that is even better, because it means the promotions aren't a high-demand service and you won't face too much competition.

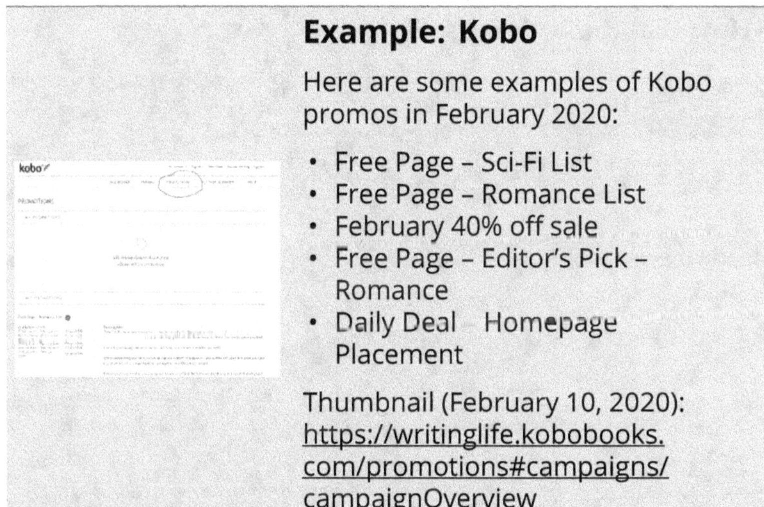

Example: Kobo

Here are some examples of Kobo promos in February 2020:

- Free Page – Sci-Fi List
- Free Page – Romance List
- February 40% off sale
- Free Page – Editor's Pick – Romance
- Daily Deal   Homepage Placement

Thumbnail (February 10, 2020): https://writinglife.kobobooks. com/promotions#campaigns/ campaignOverview

Application

> Publish your ebook directly through https://writinglife. kobobooks.com/.

> Make sure you have the promotions tab available (if not, request access through Support).

> Pick one of the promotions, ideally within the categories where promotions are offered and can be applied for your book.

Resources

> Using Promotions to Sell More Books on Kobo: https://kobowritinglife.zendesk.com/hc/en-us/articles/360002502933-Using-Promotions-to-Sell-More-Books-on-Kobo

> Dashboard Promotions Tab: How the Money Works: https://kobowritinglife.zendesk.com/hc/en-us/articles/115002501414-Dashboard-Promotions-Tab-How-the-Money-Works

TACTIC 25

THE UPSELL PRODUCT TACTIC (INFINITE SELLING LOOPS)

Description

Here's a fact that may surprise you: in 2006, Amazon was already reporting that 35% of its revenue came directly from **cross sales and upsells**.

Cross sales and upsells are a crucial channel for getting profitable, especially in markets with low profit margins like the book industry. Think about the uphill battle you face trying to make a profit: you only earn a few dollars per book on royalties, then you have ad costs and truly little room for investing to make sales—and that is all apart from the costs of labor and other expenses. I am constantly working to help authors and publishers increase their profits.

Competition in the book world is growing every day, favoring marketers who already have top-ranking books, outstanding content, or the deepest pockets. Speaking of deep pockets, this is where upsells come into play. Picture marketer A, who has a profit margin of $50 from selling a paid course at the back end. Now picture marketer B, who has no upsell product and a profit margin of only, say, $2. From a raw economic standpoint, marketer A can easily outspend marketer B on paid advertising while continuing to invest more in improving his product and marketing. Of the two, marketer A clearly has the advantage.

That is why I encourage all my authors and publishers to offer upsell products, like related books, companion courses, or affiliate products. You can dramatically increase your profit margins and your room for investing and advertising.

Examples of Success

Example: Robert Neckelius

In this free course (free at the time of writing), Robert Neckelius, author of the 4-hour agency, describes how his team can sell a few hundred $5 books a day and turn over a massive profit through upsell products.

Thumbnail (February 10, 2020): https://get.automaticclients.com/access

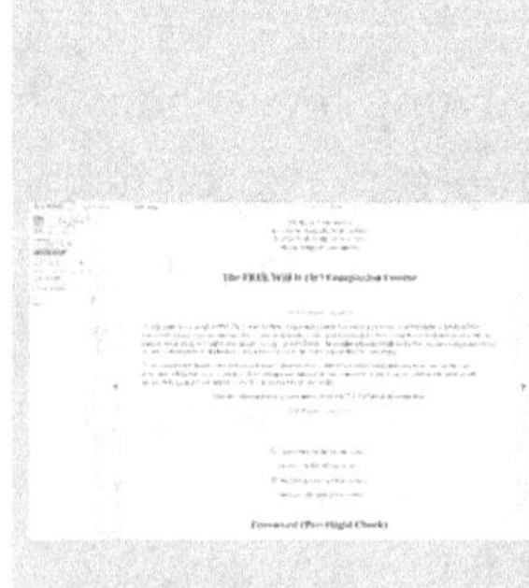

Example: Pat Flynn

Like business author Pat Flynn, you can use the first few pages of your Amazon book (visible to readers using the "Look Inside" feature) to get people to your webpage. You can also list other books at the end of your book to give readers an offer to buy more from you.

Thumbnail (February 10, 2020): https://www.amazon.com/Will-Test-Business-Waste-Money/dp/0997082305

Application

> Make a list of potential upsells relevant to your book that you would be able to deliver.

> Start with simple upsells, like affiliate links to related books or products on Amazon.

> Create your own upsell products, such as other books, companion video courses, book bundles, or coaching offers.

> Remember, you do not need to have your upsell products ready yet to start leading readers down the trail. It is just like taking pre-orders: you can create a pre-order for an upcoming book on Amazon, generating buzz and sales even if you will not be publishing it for another 12 months.

> Have the mindset of never closing the loop. Ideally, you will always have another offer for readers at stages where they would normally assume the process is closed—for example, when they've finished the book, subscribed to your email list, or sent you an email. Always give them something else. Keep the loop going.

Resources

> 15 Upselling Tips & Examples Proven to Boost Average Order: Value:
> https://optinmonster.com/upselling-tips-and-examples/

> 7 Best Examples of Upsells to Help You Maximize Your Sales:
> https://www.autogrow.co/best-upsell-examples/

> How To Boost Ecommerce Sales With Upselling:
> https://cxl.com/blog/upselling-techniques/

TACTIC 26

BOOK REVIEW AUTOMATION
[BONUS I]

Description

As I wrote in *Book Marketing Secrets*, "Reviews are the lifeblood of books in the digital age." That is why this bonus tactic might be the most powerful of them all. Without reviews you will not be selling many books—maybe none!

And yet, anyone who has tried to promote their books online knows how hard it is to get reviews. Book sales largely depend on the quantity and quality of reviews, but most buyers just will not take the time to write one. They might if they got something in return—but unfortunately, Amazon forbids incentivizing reviews in its Terms of Service (ToS).

That is where Tactic 26 comes in with a nifty little workaround—one that is compliant with Amazon's rules. Here is the secret: instead of asking for a review, you ask customers for personal feedback by email. In exchange you offer a bonus, such as a free short story or a piece of advice. And when you give them the gift, you ask if they would be so kind as to copy-paste the feedback they have already written into a review post. Clever, right? It is easy for the customer—and perfectly within the bounds of the ToS.

Think of everything you accomplish by using this one simple tactic:

❯ You get feedback from readers on how to improve your work.

❯ You establish personal contact with your readers/ reviewers.

❯ You get to thank your engaged readers with a gift.

❯ You set up a sure-fire mechanism for getting reviews that doesn't violate Amazon's ToS.

❯ Most importantly, you get more book reviews!

And you do all of this without having to invest in another service or technology. All it takes is your email account and a ready gift that will make your most loyal readers happy. Try it. You will be amazed by the results.

If you are working with a bigger audience, I recommend setting up a dedicated email address (e.g., feedback@ author.com) and creating automated responses. Alternatively, send your readers to a landing page where they can submit their feedback and email address to receive the bonus. This has the added benefit of building an email list of your reviewers.

Examples of Success

Example: Thank-You Gift on my own webpage at albertgriesmayr. com: https://www. albertgriesmayr.com/ thank-you

Application

> Prepare a bonus for readers who give you feedback on your book.

> Clearly communicate to your readers that there is a bonus for feedback available by including a "Call to Action" in your book's back or front matter. Add your contact details so readers can get in touch and take advantage of the offer.

> If you have a bigger audience than you can manage through personal communications, simplify the process by sending your readers to a landing page and setting up automated emails.

> Offer a variety of ways (besides Amazon reviews) for people to share publicly the feedback they sent you— they can post it on Audible, Goodreads, your website, or other forums.

> It is good to ask your readers for reviews, but don't push them. Remember, the personal feedback itself is already valuable! If you apply this tactic, be OK with not getting a post from everybody.

Resources

> ❯ How to get Book Reviews in 2020:
> https://www.slideshare.net/griesmayr/how-to-get-
> book-reviews-2020-edition

TACTIC 27

GETTING BOOK REVIEWS WITH PUBBY.CO
[BONUS II]

Description

It is no secret that getting reviews is one of the most challenging activities for self-published authors. For new authors and authors who are not comfortable engaging with their network, promoting their books actively, or being physically located in the United States with a reliable system to tap, this can be especially challenging.

However, we all know that a book with zero reviews will likely make zero sales. So, for years, the focus was on investing in having book launch teams, engaging review generation services like Booksirens or Hiddengemsbooks, and compiling lists of power reviewers to contact.

Those activities often resulted in a good launch in which 5-10 reviews were gathered that helped the book to grow from that base. However, this process often turned out to be time-consuming and difficult.

In 2019, a new service emerged, called <u>Pubby.co</u>. Pubby helps authors get reviews by supporting other authors and earning snaps. Snaps are Pubby's currency that you can use to post your books and to get them reviewed by others.

The advantages of Pubby are as follows:

> You have full control of when and how often to get reviewed.

> You can support other authors and earn snaps to have your books read and reviewed by peers.

> You can get reviews for books within 5-10 days, making book launches or preparations for book promotions far easier.

> You save time and money by reducing efforts to contact book reviewers by email or via social media.

I tested Pubby extensively, and I have been part of publishing groups who have done the same. So, in today's market, it is safe to say that Pubby is a truly helpful service for getting book reviews. It might even be the secret weapon for book authors in 2020.

You can learn more about how Pubby works and get a 15% discount by clicking the following link: https://pubby.co/?invite=5101

Examples of Success

Example: Book Launch of Kids Activity Book "Get This Book Wet" | Getting review count to 5 in a matter of days.

In 2020, I published a kids activity book on Amazon, and solely relied on Pubby for getting the first reviews. It worked well, and within a matter of days I had 5 reviews, that allowed me to start Amazon ads and to look for further promotion opportunities. https://www.amazon.com/Get-This-Book-Wet-Experimenting/dp/B08CJNYJY8

Example: Getting Reviews for Book Marketing Secrets [Backlist Book Project]

Earlier in 2020 I had published Book Marketing Secrets, but never really started promoting it on Amazon. The results were little sales and little reviews on Amazon. By posting the book, I quickly added a couple of reviews as well.

https://www.amazon.com/Book-Marketing-Secrets-fundamental-self-publishing-ebook/dp/B083CVHGV9

Application

> Start reviewing books on Amazon yourself and start earning snaps on Pubby.

> Launch a new book with the help of Pubby, and get your first 5 reviews quickly, when reviewing books of other authors and earning snaps.

> Use Pubby to grow review count for previously published books (both successful books and books that might need a new push).

> Prepare for the ultimate book launch, by earning lots of snaps before your book launches, to have lots of snaps to invest.

> Help fellow authors by sharing Pubby with them and helping them growing review count more quickly.

Resources

> Get Reviewers [Pubby.co]
> http://tarrantsmith.com/2020/02/11/get-reviewers/

> The new way to get book reviews: A look at 'Pubby'
> https://deviancepress.com/2019/05/21/the-new-way-to-get-book-reviews-a-look-at-pubby/

> Pubby Review [2020] – Video
> https://www.youtube.com/watch?v=cGyd-_F8AAw

TACTIC 28

USING LIBRARYBUB
[BONUS III]

Description

2020 has been a year for libraries. When you look at the numbers [include them], 2020 has brought a big increase in readership for libraries. LibraryBub is a service that enables authors to reach all important libraries throughout the United States by one single email.

I have successfully used this with my own clients in 2020 so it is a fantastic tactic to choose. However, not all books are suitable. Make sure that you fulfill the following characteristics:

> It must be interesting for libraries.

> The book should have been on the market for some time.

> The book needs to have a strong level of credibility (especially in the form of reviews).

> It should be an established book that libraries can confidently offer to their patrons.

Examples of Success

S.L. Morgan, *Best-selling, award-winning author*

To gain exposure like this, is what every self-published author dreams of! Having our books considered by libraries only expands our opportunities to reach new readers everywhere! LibraryBub's plan to reach them is an invaluable service and every author who is considering this service should jump on board without reservations! Thank you, LibraryBub! This service exceeded my expectations!

S.L Morgan reporting on Librarybub: Screenshot taken on 1/14/2021 from: http://librarybub.com/librarybub-authors-feature/

Dina Colman, *Best-selling, award-winning author*

When the email was sent out to librarians, my book ("Four Quadrant Living: Making Healthy Living Your New Way of Life") had an 18% click rate. That's extraordinary in email marketing. My book received over 400 clicks, which means that hundreds of librarians were interested in my book. I thought it was a big win to get my book into my local library. I'm very excited about the possibility of my book being in even more libraries across the country. LibraryBub helped make this happen for me!

Dina Colman reporting on Librarybub, Screenshot taken on 1/14/2021 from: http://librarybub.com/librarybub-authors-feature/

Application

> LibraryBub encourages libraries to "join 10,000 happy libraries" since they work with all major libraries and are the industry's first service connecting indie and small press authors with libraries. http://librarybub.com/

> Authors can apply for a featured deal in LibraryBub's targeted weekly email that reaches over 10,000 librarians every week. http://librarybub.com/authors/

Resources

> Getting Your Book into Libraries by Eric Otis Simmons https://www.amazon.com/gp/product/1671459954

> How I Sold 80,000 Books: Book Marketing for Authors (Self-Publishing Through Amazon and Other Retailers) by Alinka Rutkowska https://www.amazon.com/HOW-SOLD-000-BOOKS-Publishing-ebook/dp/B00WWUR1O4

> Self-Publishers Toolkit: Includes Self-Publishing in the 2020s and Marketing Your Book to Libraries https://www.amazon.com/gp/product/B08C97TFXP

> Video Interview of Alinka Rutkowska, Founder of Library Bub and #1 bestselling author of more than 20 books https://www.topbusinessleaders.com/alinka-rutkowska-outsource-your-book/

TACTIC 29

USING PATREON
[BONUS IV]

Description

Patreon is a platform where creative people can be found and supported. For authors, this is an excellent way to share book projects. The amazing thing is that you can build a monthly subscription system with basically zero technical skills. Patreon is focused on authors and creative projects in general.

Examples of Success

Zach Weinersmith

is creating SMBC Comics and Books

Example: Zack Weinersmith

Zach Weinersmith lists five different levels of giving in the amounts of $1, $3, $5, $10, and $100. Authors offer things like early access to their work. For instance, since Zach is also a comic illustrator, at the $5 and above level, Zach takes drawing requests in a half-hour live webcast. At the time of this writing, he has over 3200 supporters and is receiving over $6800 per month. That is impressive.

https://www.patreon.com/ZachWeinersmith

© Thumbnail/Screenshot, January 2021

Example: Nicolas Lietzau

Nicolas Lietzau named his different levels of support all with memorable names (that may have to do with the Enderal Trilogy he is requesting financial support to write): 1) Nefarious Nihilist ($2/month), 2) Cantankerous Cynic ($5/month), 3) Passionate Pragmatist ($10/month), 4) Hard-boiled Hedonist ($25/month), 5) Inebriated Idealist ($45/month), 6) Uncouth Utopist ($90/month), and 7) Vociferous Visionary ($250/month). At the highest level of support, Nicolas includes a personal call with him to discuss the novel, writing, or anything that comes to mind. This is a great offer for his fans. At this writing, he has over 125 supporters and receives over $1100 in support. Nicolas is a published author who is continuing to write fiction books.

https://www.patreon.com/niseam

© Thumbnail/Screenshot, January 2021

Application

> Describe in detail what it is you write about. Be creative. Remember, you are trying to motivate others to financially support you. It also helps to share a few personal details about yourself. For example, you could mention the name of your loyal pet companion and a short description about their personality and what it is they do while you write.

> Share a professional picture of yourself as well as any images (that you have permission to share) which are related to your writing project. This helps others connect to what you are doing.

> Think about your writing goals as well as the level of support you want and the level you would like to have. Decide how many giving levels you would like to offer and what you can include as a gift back to them.

Resources

> The Crowdfunding Guide for Authors and Writers by Judith Briles (Winner of the USA Best Book Award) https://www.amazon.com/CrowdFunding-Guide-Authors-Writers/dp/1885331576

> The Poet and Writer's Complete Guide to Being A Writer: Everything You Need to Know About Craft, Inspiration, Agents, Editors, Publishing, and the Business of Building a Sustainable Writing Career by Kevin Larimer and Mary Gannon https://www.amazon.com/Poets-Writers-Complete-Guide-Writer/dp/1982123079

TACTIC 30

BUILDING TRAFFIC, CREDIBILITY AND YOUR NETWORK THROUGH THE MAGIC 100 [BONUS V]

Description

Russell Brunson originally coined the term, "Dream 100". For Russell Brunson, the Dream 100 is coming up with a list of 100 influencers with whom you would love to collaborate. The idea is to carefully research influential bloggers, business owners, or anyone with a strong following or shared mindset. Then you should build a relationship with each of these 100 people so that you have access to them before you need it.

The concept is great, as it allows to jumpstart your audience and make powerful shortcuts to the top. In today's digital landscape, it does take a lot of time, to go from 0 to the top. Thus, it is much smarter using aggregators or influencers to build an audience and to attract attention quicker.

The concept of the MAGIC 100 is like Russell Brunson's Dream 100; however, it has one major tweak. It contains to not only look for people with an audience of influence, but you also look for channels, websites, and articles with existing traffic, where you potentially could be featured.

So, with the MAGIC 100, we are not only looking for influencers, but also popular sources on the web (such as Quora posts, blog articles, and Google snippets) that might provide an opportunity for us to be recommended.

Examples of Success

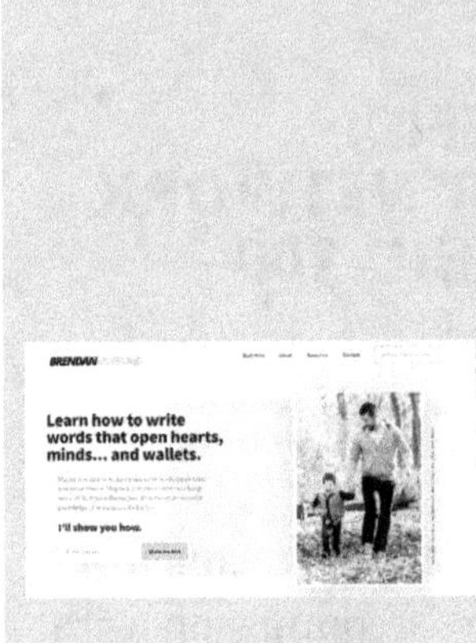

Example: Brendon Hufford

Brendon Hufford is an expert in SEO and states that Russell Brunson's Dream 100 have been pivotal, in building his business. Check out the video below, to learn about his experiences and applications for applying the Dream 100 (with a focus on link building, like suggested in the Magic 100).

https://youtu.be/MvhqG7gNs7Y

© Thumbnail/Screenshot from brendonhuffard.com, January 2021

Example: Novelify | Albert Griesmayr

When re-launching Novelify in early 2021, I decided to build upon my previous contacts from my Magic 500, as well as adding new traffic targets with success

https://www.novelify.com

© Thumbnail/Screenshot from novelify.com, January 2021

Application

> Research at least 50 influencers (within your niche) with whom you would love to work. Choose those who have a strong following and who would be a true gamer changer if they decide to support you.

> Research 50 channels and/or unique articles/videos/ websites within your niche, that have strong existing traffic (e.g., come up at rank 1-3 for your main keywords via a Google search, have the most subscribers on YouTube, come up on top of a YouTube search, etc.). They might be blog articles, Wikipedia pages, social media sources, videos, etc.

> Reach out to the 50 influencers on one hand, and on the other hand, try to be featured on your 50 target sites.

> Focus on the long game. Seek to build a relationship with your Magic 100 first, before asking them for favors or bluntly promoting your content.

Resources

- The Dream 100 by Russell Brunson — Podcast
  https://marketingsecrets.com/the-dream-100-part-1-of-3/

- The Concept of the Dream 100
  https://medium.com/@donaldlee50/the-concept-of-the-dream-100-af471e76afee

- Dream 100 — The Ultimate Tactic for Exploding Your Business
  https://brendanhufford.com/dream-100/

- The Ultimate White Hat Link Building Technique NOBODY Tells You — Video
  https://www.youtube.com/watch?v=MvhqG7gNs7Y

TACTIC 31

INCREASE BOOK RANKINGS WITH A CASHBACK CAMPAIGN [BONUS VI]

Description

Book launches can be doomed to fail without proper preparation. Failing to get into Amazon's SEO rankings can mean your work fades into obscurity very quickly.

This is why we suggest having a marketing tactic which gives you control over your initial book sales and grabs your readers' attention.

Cashback services is one of these tactics. Cashback services allow you to give potential readers a discount of your choice on your book, providing them an offer they can't possibly refuse.

Competition is getting fiercer and fiercer on Amazon and there are already quite a few examples of cashback services out there. Most of them do not apply to Kindle eBooks. Fortunately, we've managed to find one that does and which has proven itself to be successful: Massview by Snagshout.

Examples of Success

Example: The Love Hex [Book Launch]

The book launch of The Love Hex, was supported by a small Snagshout campaign, distributing 10 ebooks for free, making sure to get initial sales in the first couple of days.

https://www.snagshout.com/offers/the-love-hex-or-nicest-flings-in-mexico-eb/3b20220

© Thumbnail/Screenshot from snagshout.com, January 2021

Example: The Photographer's Field Guide [Ranking Campaign]

We needed the ebook for the Photographer's field guide to sell initially, in order to get results from an AMS ad campaign. By running a snagshout campaign, we helped Amazon to notice the book, and subsequently ads started to show up and produce results.

https://www.snagshout.com/offers/ebook-the-landscape-photographer-s-field/2be4be4

© Thumbnail/Screenshot from snagshout.com, January 2021

Application

> Firstly, support your book launch by setting it up on Massview, offer readers a discount or even offer your book for free.

> It is recommended to run this campaign on a month where your book is already discounted (e.g. its launch month)

> Some services offer to add custom URLs with rankings, do not choose this option though as it is against Amazon's TOS.

> Some services offer to ask purchasers for posting reviews later. This can be a very useful additional feature. Make sure that this process is not incentivized though, in order to comply with Amazon TOS.

Resources

> Myth Busters: Are Amazon Product Launch Websites Bad for FBA Sellers?
https://www.junglescout.com/blog/amazon-product-launch-websites-bad-for-fba/

> Paul Johnson of Massview: Five Strategies I Used To Grow My Business To Reach Seven Figures In Revenue
https://medium.com/authority-magazine/paul-johnson-of-massview-five-strategies-i-used-to-grow-my-business-to-reach-seven-figures-in-42df4b58aef2

TACTIC 32

Use Google Play Books Promo Code Campaigns To Generate Buzz

Description

Google Play Books recently launched promo code campaigns, which can be used to offer select customers a discounted print book, ebook or audiobook without lowering the list price.

As an author or publisher offering books through Google Play Books, you can create up to 5,000 codes per campaign and up to 3 promo code campaigns per month.

Nate Hoffelder of the *Digital Reader* described this new feature and a "good development" and "another reason to set up an author/publisher account in their bookstore."

Google Books recently updated their terms of service and have increased their royalty split to 70% in 60+ countries from 52%, showing that they are serious players in the publishing game.

Recommendations

Recommendation: How To Sell Books In 2020

PublishDrive highly recommends using Google Play Books in 2020 going into 2021 with this very informative video.

https://www.youtube.com/watch?v=2rT0GyrgY3w

© Thumbnail/Screenshot from www.youtube.com, January 2021

Recommendation: Google Play Books, Is It Worth It?

In this video by Self Publishing With Dale, he covers Google Play Books and the benefits of choosing it over rival services such as Amazon Publishing or Kobo books.

https://www.youtube.com/watch?v=HXQMra_qwbo&ab_channel=Self-PublishingwithDale

© Thumbnail/Screenshot from www.youtube.com, January 2021

Application

> Firstly, sign up to Google Books if you haven't done so already. Click <u>here</u> to do so

> Upload titles and start a promo code campaign.

> Choose which discount you would like to offer readers: Offer your book for FREE, for a DISCOUNTED PERCENTAGE or a DISCOUNTED FIXED PRICE.

> You can use up to 5,000 promo codes and up to 3 campaigns per month.

Resources

> The Digital Reader: Google Play Books now pays a 70% Royalty in 60+ Countries. https://the-digital-reader.com/2020/10/13/google-play-books-now-pays-a-70-royalty-in-60-countries/

> Google Play Books Unveils Promo Code Campaigns. https://goodereader.com/blog/digital-publishing/google-play-books-unveils-promo-code-campaigns

★ 4 — CHEATSHEET ★

BOOK SALES EXPLOSION CHEATSHEET
DISCOVER ALL 32 BOOK MARKETING TACTICS AT A GLANCE

1) BOOK SALES FUNNELS

2) LOOK INSIDE BONUS

3) FREE PRINT BOOK

4) ALEXA SKILLS

5) AFFILIATE MARKETING

6) NEW FORMATS & TRANSL.

7) KICKSTARTER FUNDING

8) CIALDINIFY YOUR BOOK

9) PERMAFREE EBOOK

10) MATCHING COVERS

11) IRRESISTIBLE BONUSES

12) PRE-ORDER TACTIC

13) AMAZON BESTSELLER

14) PINTEREST TRAFFIC

15) EMAIL MARKETING

16) COLLABORATION

17) VIDEO MARKETING

18) AMAZON SELECT +

19) AUTHORITY PUBLISHING

20) SIMPLE AMAZON SEO

21) AMAZON AMS ADS

22) AUDIOBOOK CREATION

23) RETARGETING

24) KOBO PUBLISHING

25) UPSELL PRODUCTS

26) BOOK REVIEW AUTOM.

27) REVIEWS VIA PUBBY

28) USING LIBRARYBUB

29) USING PATREON

30) THE MAGIC 100

31) CASHBACK CAMPAIGNS

32) GOOGLE PLAY

www.albertgriesmayr.com

5 — EPILOGUE
LOOKING BEYOND 2020

"The biggest room in the world is the room for improvement."
Harvey Mackay

Dear Writer,

I want to finish this book with a quote by one of my former clients, 7-time New York Times bestselling author Harvey Mackay. He hit the nail on the head when he said, "The biggest room in the world is the room for improvement." This quote became one of his most memorable and has been re-shared by thousands of people around the world.[6]

I absolutely love this quote because it always reminds me of the road ahead. Even good products should never be seen as completely finished; otherwise, they'll become obsolete faster than you can blink.

------

6   Source: Google the quote and you get tens of thousands of search results. Some sources also cite German statesman Helmut Schmidt as the original source, others share the quote with source anonymous.

That is why I will certainly be updating this book over time and creating new editions if better tactics and strategies emerge.[7] Furthermore, I recommend you do the same with your own books.

Do not see them as finished, but keep on improving, make them masterpieces, and all your marketing efforts will be easier as well.

I truly hope that this book was of high value to you and that you have learned tactics you'll be able to apply in your marketing—and more importantly, that these tactics will help you multiply your book sales.

In case you haven't taken a look at Scribando (www. scribando.com) yet, I highly recommend doing so. My service will help you stay not only up to date on what is happening in the market but also informed about the latest success strategies for how to sell books.

In the end, to hit the jackpot as an author, you need to master both areas: timeless book marketing knowledge + the latest success strategies. With this book + Scribando, you have the perfect knowledge setup for selling lots of books.

I also invite you to look at the surprise gift that I have prepared for you. It will also help you grow your career as an author. In addition, when you sign up on my webpage, you will be in touch with me and will not miss any new releases or book marketing insights.

---

7   If you know of a book promotion tactic that should be in this book, don't be shy! Reach out to me. I'll certainly reward contributions that find their way into updated book editions.

As a writer, you'll also gain insight into how important it is to get reviews. I like to say that "reviews are the lifeblood of books in the digital age."

That's why I would also be super happy to receive a review of this book from you.

Finally, let me close this book by sharing one last insight with you that has been quite valuable to me in recent years. It comes from the German saying "Der stete Tropfen höhlt den Stein," which means "Constant dripping wears the stone."

When I started following this simple principle and applying it to my business in various areas, my performance began to improve significantly. It is important to be involved in something for the long run, to put continuous and concentrated effort into fewer things and to create routines and realistic plans for achieving what is profoundly important to you.

That is a core principle that I follow and apply in my own business, and I am sure that if you apply it, you will improve your results as well. You do not always need to create new books, new projects, offers, or features. Nor do you need to change careers or whole businesses to become—and stay—successful.

Instead, focus on what you already have, polish it, and develop it until it shines like a diamond—a product that you are proud of and that your customers will want to have.

Writing this book was a pleasure to me, because I did what I love to do: share my knowledge on book marketing with you. With that, I wish you all the best in your publishing career.

Best Wishes,

Albert Griesmayr
Vienna, January 1, 2021

★ **THE END** ★

www.ingramcontent.com/pod-product-compliance
Lightning Source LLC
Chambersburg PA
CBHW061348250726
48657CB00004B/1386